Gunning for Upland Birds and Wildfowl

D0065128

Tom Hennessey

Gunning for Upland Birds and Wildfowl

by Shirley E. Woods, Jr.

illustrated by Tom Hennessey

Winchester Press

Jacket and Book Design by Marcy J. Katz

Library of Congress Cataloging in Publication Data

Woods, Shirley E
Gunning for upland bird and wildfowl.
Includes index.
1. Fowling. I. Title.
SK313.W66   799.2′4   75-34232
ISBN 0–87691–219–6

Published by Winchester Press
205 East 42nd Street, New York 10017

Printed in the United States of America

Second printing   1976

WINCHESTER is a Trademark of Olin Corporation
used by Winchester Press, Inc. under authority
and control of the Trademark Proprietor.

Contents

Introduction

Show me a man who his companions all respect in forest, field or lake or stream and I have found a man who knows his way around the marshes, woodcock covers and the trout and salmon rivers.

Show me a friendly man whose casts are long and accurate, who ties his flies and lends a hand to fishermen less practiced in the angler's art; a man with whom it is a privilege to share a blind or watch him bring a partridge tumbling stone dead from the autumn sky; a man concerned, despite his youthful peccadilloes, honestly confessed and as honestly repented, with conservation and the welfare of the people that he meets, be they guides or fellow sportsmen; a man who often smiles and sometimes laughs at what a lesser man would call misfortune. Such a man should write a book; he has.

Here Shirley Woods has given us a chance to read with pleasure—and with profit too—about the people, places and the things we love; to read some evening by the fire when the snow surrounds our dwelling and the song birds have gone south. The book deserves our reading yet again when game birds nest and rods are taken out of winter storage; when violets flower by the brooks and salmon seek home rivers after feeding far at sea. The author is as able with his pen as with a Churchill side by side or Winston rod. You'll like him, like his story, like the pictures that he paints and like his book; what is more, you'll learn a lot; I have.

Dana S. Lamb

This book is dedicated to
my late father
Shirley E. Woods
who set me on the road,
and to my brother
John R. Woods
who has been my companion
on the rewarding journey

Preface

This book was born of a number of diaries—and the need to do something about them. Initially, the idea was to have the contents typed verbatim and bound into a single volume. The project then evolved into its present form—a chronological resume composed of excerpts reinforced where necessary with background information. Most of the episodes occur during the past 25 years. While this is a memoir, I have tried to highlight the significant points that have helped me in the hunting of each species. These are included for your consideration, in the hope that some may be of help to you, too.

The original object was to preserve and document memories. Therefore, while some of the stories may appear fanciful, *all* are based on fact and, in some cases, names have been changed for obvious reasons.

My brother John and I were born with a silver (sporting) spoon, but lost it when Dad died in 1954. We were left with a love for the outdoors, a champagne taste in the pursuit of sport, and a beer income. In a sense, we went back to square one. Prior to Dad's death we had enjoyed luxury shooting with little thought required on our part, as everything was "laid on" for us. In 1955, as young men, we had neither the money nor the knowledge to achieve good sport. In addition, many welcome mats disappeared with chilling suddenness. We were on our own.

The diaries record our many follies; if there was a mistake to be made, we made it. This book may help the novice avoid some of the pitfalls and amuse the experienced. After making every possible error, Fate has usually relented and we have realized some measure of success. In a sense, we were lucky as we had no comfortable base to hold us in our quest for good hunting, and our restless roamings have exposed us to a rich variety of sport. In the process we have made some wonderful friends. The ensuing pages may imply that I am a steely-eyed Nimrod and paragon of virtue. This is not so. The truth is that I have missed countless birds, and on one memorable occasion, shot so badly that my dog turned his back on me and howled.

Successful gameshooting is both an art and a science; technical skill must be combined with a knowledge of the quarry. Long runs at skeet require flawless technique and intestinal fortitude, but all factors are predetermined and there is no element of surprise. Gameshooting, on the other hand, has many variables which make the technical factor a relatively minor part of the equation. First, there is the problem of locating the game; and second, as each species has differing flight characteristics, it is vital to know what to expect when the bird glides into range or erupts from the grass. The crisp execution of the shot is dependent upon your knowledge of the variables.

Initially, when I went afield the object was to kill as much game as possible. In the intervening years, I have come to realize that our birds are a diminishing resource to be appreciated rather than exploited. While shooting is a favorite pastime, the criterion of a good outing is no longer the size of the bag; rather, it is the overall enjoyment of the day.

Finally, you may disagree with some opinions and/or consider them ill-founded. It is worth noting that these opinions are the product of the most demanding school in the world, the school of experience.

In writing this book I have had to relive the incidents as they occurred, and this has provided great pleasure. I hope you will enjoy them too.

—S.E.W.

Tom Hennessey

chapter 1

The Black Bay Duck Club

The Ottawa River forms the boundary between the provinces of Ontario and Quebec. The river has always been a major flyway for the black duck. The north shore or Quebec side, from the town of Masson to the village of Plaisance, is marked by numerous shallow bays and edged with miles of marsh grass. This section provides a quality of duck shooting unsurpassed in eastern Canada.

As bees are drawn to honey so hunters were attracted to the Ottawa River. Not only "locals," but gunners from nearby Ottawa and Montreal maneuvered for a stake in the fabulous shooting. This jostling and crowding resulted in numerous skirmishes amounting to a full scale "marsh war" which simmered into the 1920's. During that decade, virtually all the choice property was purchased or leased by syndicates or individuals from Montreal and Ottawa. Each syndicate or club maintained an armed neutrality with its neighbor and enforced their territorial rights through trusted guardians.

These guardians were recruited from roughly a dozen prolific French families, and while they wore no distinctive livery, they were well known and recognized for their particular loyalty. Frequently sons succeeded fathers in service. To a man, they were farm bred, had spent a lot of time on the river, and knew ducks.

With the choice areas posted, the casual or itinerant hunter had no place to shoot unless he poached — a hazardous business. While one may deplore, in this democratic age, the denial of sport to the average citizen and the triumph of the privileged few, the ducks flourished due to the reduced gunning pressure. Each club provided a resting or sanctuary area within its respective boundaries to maintain a good supply of resident birds. Knowing that ducks need food as well as cover, wild rice, sago and pond weed were hand planted. Today we would call this "environmental awareness." There is good reason to believe that the planted foods were augmented by an impressive tonnage of bagged grain (particularly buckwheat) during the shooting season. Unspoken rivalry existed among the clubs to see which could attract and hold the most birds. This enlightened self-interest guaranteed easy limits each weekend but the kill as a *percentage* of the total waterfowl population was small.

Through the years the clubs continued to nibble at each other's boundaries; particularly if an adjoining property was subject to lease rather than owned outright. Some farmers did very well playing one off against the other, and one singularly venal character would, after short-leasing to the highest bidder, further augment his income by clandestine daily rentals of the *same* pond to selected friends.

The Black Bay Duck Club was located on the Ottawa River near Thurso. The property (roughly 1000 acres) was a duck shooter's paradise.

The white wood clubhouse and outbuildings were situated on a peninsula connected to civilization by a short causeway and one mile of twisting private road. Opposite the camp, in the center of the river (one mile wide at this point) was fabled Horseshoe Island. The island, named for its crescent shape, embraced a shallow 20-acre pond. This slough would, on occasion, have so many black ducks that the entire surface would be covered, and the roar as they rose could never be forgotten. River blinds at each end of the island provided superb late season shooting for puddlers and diving ducks.

Standing on the front porch, the river and the Horseshoe were before you; looking to the rear, a broad inland marsh stretched from east to west, intersected by the causeway. To the west was marsh grass as far as the eye could see; this vista was punctuated by four well-spaced ponds hidden among the reeds. To the east, from the causeway, was a narrow grasslined canal known as the Snellier. The Snellier was a much favored flight line for teal and ringbills, particularly in the evening. On the eastern boundary, two large, tree-lined sloughs offered a refuge for blacks during heavy weather. To the north, east, and west, were many acres of productive upland cover, making a limit of woodcock a routine occurrence.

The Clubhouse proper consisted of a large central living room with picture windows overlooking the river and the inland marsh. Wings extended east and west from the living room with a drying room leading to the back door. The east wing housed four double bedrooms; the west wing the dining room, kitchen, and cook's bedroom. Cooking was done on a wood stove, heat was provided by the open brick fireplace in the living room and an ancient box stove in the drying room. Light came from suspended oil lamps and the only touch of luxury, indoor plumbing, was operated by a gas engine. There was no telephone.

The bedrooms had built-in bunk beds with innerspring mattresses covered by Hudson Bay blankets and plain sheets. At the foot of each member's bed was his sleeping bag, reserved for late season use. A chest of drawers, chair and mirror completed the furnishings.

The living room had an old oak card table in the center surrounded by six comfortable chairs. On each side of the fireplace were the prints "To Hit is History" "To Miss is Mystery." Each wall had a beautifully mounted pair of game birds in glass and walnut exhibition frames. The dining room had a full length picture window and a table which would seat ten people comfortably. The drying room had the gun rack, rows of pegs for coats and hats as well as built-in drawers running down the west wall. The center of the room was occupied by a wood burning stove and in one corner were the wash basin and water closet. The most notable decoration was a sun-faded print by A. B. Frost, "Rail Shooting."

Across the driveway stood the guardian's house, two barns, and a large storage shed. Boat docks at the front and rear completed the picture. Tall elms flanked the settlement.

I have not mentioned kennels, as the dogs were permitted to run free and lived summer and winter in the crawl space beneath the clubhouse. This may sound rather casual, but the dogs were always fit and didn't appear to suffer even though the thermometer might register −35° in midwinter.

The principals of the club were John J. Heney, James C. H. Bonbright and my father, Shirley E. Woods.

Jack Heney, some years older than the other two, was elected president. To this post he brought an uncanny knowledge of ducks, the ability to shoot straight, and a devastating sense of humor.

Jamie Bonbright of Rochester was, at the time, First Secretary to the U.S. Ambassador in Ottawa. In the ensuing years, frequent absences, due to postings, limited his participation in the club's affairs. However, this was more than compensated for by his generous annual invitation to Jack and Dad to fish salmon at his camp on the Grand Cascapedia.

Dad, a pioneer in the manufacture of outdoor clothing and sleeping bags, loved the outdoors. Like Jack, he knew ducks and was a superb shot. His generosity and kindness made him a legion of friends. Possibly due to his fluency in French, the day-to-day running of the club fell on his shoulders.

To illustrate the modus operandi of the Black Bay Duck Club, imagine we are there on a typical October weekend in the late 1940's.

Jack Heney, taking a taxi from nearby Ottawa, has arrived at the camp late Friday morning, and spent the afternoon making a thorough reconnaissance of the duck situation. Dad and the others check in during the afternoon, and the last arrive by sundown.

The conversation around the fire before dinner is of ducks and pending weather rather than the Dow Jones averages or the Berlin Airlift. At 7:30, Mrs. Higgins, the cook, announces that dinner is ready. Quite possibly our move to the dining room is delayed by another round of cocktails. Mrs. Higgins, a handsome, full-blooded Iroquois Indian can not only cook a roast of beef to a turn, but by some magic, suspend the moment so that if her "boys" (as she privately refers to them) are an hour late the meat retains its savor. Her good humor and sparkling smile light up the kitchen.

After dinner, the guardian, Fern Legault, comes in and

discusses the morrow with Father and Jack. As a result of their consultation, Jack assigns blinds for the next morning; this is his prerogative as President, and a custom of long standing.

By 11 P.M. the camp is dark and still, except for the flickering light of the dying embers in the fireplace.

Before daylight, a muted clatter in the drying room signals that Fern is stoking the Quebec Heater. Moments later the kindling crackles as the living room fire roars to life. Footsteps come down the hall, stop in front of your door, and a quick rap precedes the announcement "Five o'clock, Monsieur."

The icy temperature of your room is apparent as you reach out of the snug sleeping robe to light the lamp; and your breath can be seen in its warm glow. As your feet touch the frigid floor, no time is to be wasted in gathering all your clothes prior to a dash down the hall to the living room. If the fireplace is occupied, the drying room provides the necessary warmth; indeed, traffic between the two rooms is to be expected, as garments are sought or the water closet visited. By the time you are dressed you can smell bacon and eggs, and the oak table in the living room holds a tray of freshly squeezed orange juice —a nice touch as cold mornings sometimes merit a little lacing of the orange juice from the sideboard. While a "heart starter" may be in order, the unwritten rule is no drinking in the blind; and this is strictly observed.

Following breakfast, all hands file out the back door to meet Fern and the guides. As a guest, you meet your guide and notice that his last name is Legault; not surprising, as he is one of Fern's brothers or cousins.

Your guide then picks up one or two large tin suitcases and leads the way to your boat or truck. The "suitcases" are in fact special containers for the decoys, which are black duck skins mounted over a cork base.

These "feather" decoys were peculiar to the Lower

Ottawa and came into being as a result of the ban on the use of live decoys. The originator, a taxidermist named Hector Bedard, was a legendary figure noted for both his exquisite work and marvelous understanding of game. His shooting credentials were impeccable; he was not only a champion trap shot but also a former market gunner. Hector's decoys were so lifelike that when caught napping I have had to both count the spread *and* watch for movement to discern the live bird.

Upon reaching the blind your guide sets out the decoys, makes sure you are comfortable; then, with Labrador at heel, disappears into the bush. His role is to go after any long cripples immediately with the dog, but to leave birds falling close to the blind until pick up time. In this way, your shooting is not disturbed. When you are finished, you signal the guide with a wave; and he comes over to collect the rest of the bag. Your responsibility is to remember, as precisely as possible, where you dropped the birds.

Normally, all the guns are back at the camp by 11 A.M., giving one ample time to have a snooze and get cleaned up for 1 P.M. lunch. On Saturday you listen, with mounting excitement, to the fortunes of the Ottawa Rough Rider football team on the radio.

Should you want to shoot in the afternoon a fresh blind is assured, as no blinds are shot twice in the same day. The final whistle of the football game is the signal to gather your gear and depart for the evening flight.

As one might expect, the guest list, over the years, numbered many prominent figures, including foreign ambassadors, Canadian Governors-General and H.R.H. Prince Philip, Duke of Edinburgh. It was customary for guests to sign the log book and write a few words of appreciation. One cryptic notation, over the signature of a titled British diplomat remains in my memory; it read

"Masses of duck; managed to keep them at bay." On a more serious note, the original register played a part in an international spy scandal.

In November, 1945, Igor Gouzenko, a cipher clerk in the Russian Embassy in Ottawa, defected, and sought asylum of the Canadian government. The circumstances were so sensational that Hollywood subsequently produced a movie, "The Iron Curtain," starring Dana Andrews and Gene Tierney. When Gouzenko went to the R.C.M.P., he had a sheaf of top secret papers abstracted from the Embassy code room stuffed in his shirt. These documents not only revealed subversive activity in Canada, but led to the discovery of espionage rings in the U.S. and Great Britain.

During the next year the Canadian government launched a number of prosecutions based on Gouzenko's evidence. The course of justice was, however, impeded by a legal technicality concerning the signature of the Russian Military Attaché. Colonel Nikolai Zabotin, a charming former Czarist officer, was not only the Military Attaché, but clearly the master spy of the Canadian operation. His signature appeared on a number of incriminating documents, but could not be verified as he had scrupulously avoided signing any embassy guest ledgers, hotel registers etc. during his time in Canada. One of his staff always did this for him.

Father learned of the problem, and remembered that some years earlier Colonel Zabotin had been a guest at the duck camp. Indeed, after lashings of vodka and appropriate toasts to East-West friendships (plus good hunting) the Colonel had signed the guest book with a flourish.

Within hours, Dad delivered the Black Bay Duck Club log to the authorities and was subsequently required to testify. The log was kept as evidence and rests in an unknown vault of the Department of Justice to this day.

Mother always maintained that as a result of Father's participation in the Gouzenko case, the Woods family went right to the top of the NKVD "want" list!

Up to 1963, the Black Bay Duck Club provided a breeding and holding area for literally thousands of ducks, with shooting that was second to none. Sadly, this has all changed. In 1960, the Quebec government commenced expropriation proceedings to acquire all the land to be flooded from the dam site at Carillon to the town of Gatineau, a distance of nearly 50 miles. At the same time, giant timber machines started to clear the landscape along the shoreline, in preparation for a five-foot rise in the water level.

The raising of the river, combined with the cutting of timber, changed Black Bay beyond recognition. Most of the woodcock bush disappeared, the four inland ponds became one continuous lake and the Snellier turned into a reedless canal. Worst of all, the storied Horseshoe no longer attracted ducks, the wild rice was drowned out, and the only fall visitors were the odd merganser. This, where the late Larry Koller wrote in 1954 (*Argosy* magazine) that on his entrance to the pond he put up 2500 blacks and mallards! The final blow to the club was its expropriation by the provincial government. When Jack Heney signed the contract, it marked the end of an era.

Plans have just been announced by Ducks Unlimited and the Quebec government, to restore the area as a duck factory and haven for migrating birds. May they have every success!

Tom Hennessy

chapter 2

Formative Years

Up until the age of 20, virtually all my shooting was done at or near the Black Bay Duck Club; or "camp" as we referred to it. Dad was the only member with children, and as the others rarely visited the premises except in the fall, we came to regard it as our personal bailiwick during the rest of the year. Because of boarding school and seaside summer holidays, our time at the camp was fragmented, and varied from year to year. Our activities were, in a word, unstructured, we roamed the river, marsh and surrounding bush and were constantly learning something new. In retrospect, one of the great attractions of being at the camp was the freedom. Dad's permissiveness implied that we were responsible; if he worried that we might get drowned, lost or shot (all of which were possible) he never showed it.

Over the years we got to know the lay of the land intimately, the hazards of the swift Ottawa River, and the haunts of many creatures, from the muskrat houses in the Snellier to the bald eagle's next on the Horseshoe. Our days were full, and it was here that our sporting values were firmly established.

Dad took me on my first duck hunt when I was eight. Needless to say, the expedition had been anticipated with great excitement and when I was excused from school, one cold November afternoon, I could hardly contain myself.

We arrived at the club at dusk and, as the car came to a stop, from the shadows emerged three huge Labradors. Their delight at seeing us nearly bowled me over, as they jostled and wagged their greeting. Inside the camp the fire crackled merrily, and Mrs. Higgins bustled about in the living room making sure everything was just right.

Once unpacked, Dad handed me the gun I was to use, a .410 Winchester Pump, with ventilated rib. Up to this time my gunhandling had been limited to basement practice with a Daisy air rifle, so the .410 seemed both heavy and long, but above all, an object of rare beauty. I was shown how the action worked (with particular reference to the red safety button) and dry pointed it at the ducks on the wall until my arms ached. The gun was returned to the rack, and while Dad finished his drink, I emptied the box of shells and examined them with fascination. They were Imperial 3″ high brass loads, and I still remember the clean smell of the Duco varnish on the blue cardboard hulls. In those days, the fired shell also had a delicious odor.

We had what must have been a very early dinner, after which I was trundled off to bed. Once enveloped in the bulky down robe sleep came instantly. On waking the next morning I basked in the warmth of my covering, despite the near freezing temperature of the room.

Outside, the sky was gray and flurries of dry snow, blown on an east wind, whispered against my window. To this day, when I think of perfect duck weather, that's the mix that comes to mind.

Before setting out we had a brief refresher course with the .410, Dad filled a haversack with shells, two chocolate bars, and a thermos of consommé soup. We were ready to go.

As the inner ponds were frozen, we took the guardian's truck and bumped along a dirt road to the east end of the property which terminated at Baie Dubaie. A short boat ride took us across the bay to a small grass blind on the opposite shore. Late in the season Baie Dubaie attracted both divers and puddle ducks, so our decoy spread was split into a flock of a dozen blacks and, downwind, a larger number of bluebills. My chance would come when a bird lit in the decoys.

Once settled in the blind, Dad took my gun and loaded a single cartridge in the chamber. As soon as the gun was handed back I expected birds to start piling in; but this was not to be. True, there were birds in sight quite frequently, but for some reason they spurned our set and refused to land. A number did, however, pay the penalty for coming within range of Dad's tightly choked trap gun. Finally, when the chill wind was starting to extinguish the earlier glow of excitement, a duck appeared, made a brief swing and plopped in amongst the feather decoys. The moment was electric; we held our breath as we raised our heads to identify the visitor.

Completely unconcerned, a beautiful hooded merganser drake bobbed 20 yards out, with erect crest and crisply contrasting plumage. On the whispered advice to "aim at the waterline" I eased the barrel through the reeds at the top of the blind. Once in position, the gun seemed terribly heavy and the barrel kept sweeping back and forth as though of its own accord. The situation was fraught with uncertainty as far as I was concerned, but the duck continued to nonchalantly oil its feathers. After what seemed like an age the barrel started back on course, and, as it merged with the bird, I pulled the trigger. Three things happened: the recoil knocked me back on my heels, Dad's slap sent me forward, and the duck turned turtle, with yellow paddles fanning! I was thrilled.

That was the only bird that decoyed, but just before we picked up three bluebills whistled past, downwind, at least 40 yards from the blind. Dad stood up and folded each into a ball with three shots that almost blended into one. The birds had such speed that after being hit they continued on like projectiles splashing into the gray water a full ten yards from the point of impact. Ironically, I was greatly impressed by the free fall characteristics of the dead bluebills, but took the marksmanship for granted. After all, he was my *Dad*.

Jack Heney met us back at the camp and after an early lunch we took the big boat to a shore blind on the Horseshoe. The afternoon produced a lot of shooting for Dad and Jack, as flock after flock of northern redlegs worked the Snye. My role was to finish cripples, otherwise I was to stay down, and out of harm's way. There were only two cripples during the afternoon, mute testimony to the caliber of wingshooting. When we picked up the sky was pink in the west, and, silhouetted against the glow, literally thousands of birds could be seen in flight up and down the river. Sitting in the boat on the way home, flanked by Dad and Uncle Jack, with Roger our Lab at our knees, I was utterly content.

The only justification for shooting a duck in the water is when you must finish a cripple. In that case it is imperative to do the job properly. Dad's advice to aim at the waterline was sound, as it ensured the pattern *above* the waterline would strike the head and neck of the bird, while the portion below the waterline would *ricochet* in the same area. By aiming at the waterline you will still connect, even if the charge is slightly high or low.

As it is pellets in the head that count when dispatching a cripple, it is essential to have a dense pattern. This can be obtained with a tight choke, but the best solution is to use small shot. When duck hunting I always keep a few 7½ trap loads in my pocket for this purpose.

Potting a duck on the water was one thing, to shoot one on the wing was another. The next years were devoted to achieving the hallowed status of a wingshot. To this end, Dad let us have unlimited shells and left us on our own, with a minimum of instruction. The only lesson I remember was on gun safety, which was brief but most effective. We were stood in a semi-circle behind him as he fired a duck load into a cedar fence post from a distance of five feet. The resulting jagged hole spoke volumes and was never forgotten.

Most of our shooting was in the spring, particularly at Easter, and Black Bay was an exciting place to be at that time. The end of our long winter has always been signalled by the break-up of ice on the Ottawa River. At Black Bay, rafts of ducks could be seen in every direction, their bright plumage standing out against the dead grass of the marsh or grey water of the river. In addition to the ducks, flocks of Canada geese traded back and forth from the river to the newly exposed farmers' fields. Not many songbirds would have arrived but crows, grackles and blackbirds abounded. Our main quarry on spring shoots were not the canny crows but the more obliging (and numerous) blackbirds, starlings and grackles.

These birds were not protected in Canada (and still aren't at the time of writing,) so they were legal game. I have little sympathy for starlings, as they are interlopers (introduced in the U.S. in the 1880's) and drive our native songbirds away. I do feel however, that blackbirds and grackles should be protected by law. We regarded them as sporting feathered targets and shot a great many. This phase in my gunning experience I view with genuine regret.

Looking back, I realize we were very lucky to have had such an understanding and tolerant father. A typical spring shoot will illustrate this remark.

Rising before dawn we dressed in the drying room, as though going duck shooting. Members' well-worn hunting coats and hats were "borrowed" from their pegs, their full choked, long-barreled duck guns taken down from the rack. Finally, we grabbed as many boxes of shells (from Dad's supply) as we could carry. The normal complement of ammunition was a box in each front pocket and *four* in the game bag; as a result, we set off with a marked stoop or forward slant.

We departed at first light and headed along the river. It was bordered with trees, and a haven for blackbirds and grackles. To insure adequate firepower, the plug was removed from the gun, which permitted six in the magazine and one in the chamber. Though our guns were too heavy, and too choked, we compounded our handicap by insisting on high brass loads, preferably No. 4!

When a bird hove into view, the first couple of shots were by way of a salute and not expected to do mortal harm. The next three were. If we fired five shells and the bird was still airborne, the last two were more in the nature of a farewell to a worthy opponent (who, by this time, was a dwindling speck in the sky.) We covered a lot of ground and got plenty of shooting. By 9 A.M. we were usually out of ammunition. At this point we shouldered our guns (holding them by the barrel with the action open) and marched home for breakfast.

That was the way I learned to shoot 30 years ago, but today if I were to teach a youngster to handle a shotgun, I would approach the task in a very different manner.

First, I recommend a 12-, 16- or 20-gauge that is reasonably light, with a barrel length of not more than 28 inches; bored improved cylinder or skeet, certainly no tighter than modified. The shells should be standard trap or skeet loads, to minimize recoil and provide dense patterns.

Rather than shoot feathered targets, use a hand trap as the basic training aid. At first, lob slow straightaways or slightly angled birds. These are the easiest to smash and give the boy both a feel for a moving target and confidence, which are vital at the outset.

Throughout his training period, only let him have *one* shell in the gun. This will make him concentrate on shooting properly and prevent a sloppy approach. Should the young gunner take up competitive shooting at a later date, he will have developed an attitude from the start where every shot counted. The single shell is also safer.

Once the straightaways are broken consistently, have a companion throw him incoming overhead birds, from behind an old shed or barn. Finally, using the same structure for protection, fast crossing birds provide an excellent graduation exercise. This phase teaches basic gunhandling and gunpointing.

Next, to familiarize the pupil with feathered targets, go to a game farm. Here he can experience the thrill of shooting live game under controlled conditions. I recommend that the first birds be pheasants, pointed by a well-broken dog, in open cover. After a few visits, for a final polishing, choose a dry windy day (which can make the slowest ringneck move) and head for thick cover.

With clays and preserve birds under his belt *any* boy is then ready to enter a duck blind or grouse bush.

As the years passed, Dad enforced our terms of reference with greater strictness so, by the time we were in our 'teens, blackbird shooting was out and crow shooting became the logical alternative.

We approached this challenge with vigor, but a distressing lack of knowledge. At the outset we learned it was useless to try and stalk a flock of crows, because they always had a well-placed sentinel. With this in mind, we reasoned that our best plan would be to set up an ambush. Taking great care, we built an elaborate blind in a known crow bush, and then sat for a whole day waiting in vain for the crows to appear. Our failure prompted serious reflection and resulted in a further ploy which we considered a "brainwave." We knew that crows hated owls. Therefore, if we could get a stuffed owl to complement our superb blind, success would be assured. In the drying room was a pair of mounted great horned owls, and Dad let us have the larger female for our setup. Pliers swiftly removed the log base, and a harness was fashioned of fishline around her neck so that she could be suspended by a cord. With hopes refreshed, we returned the next day to the blind, and strung the owl high in an adjacent elm.

The morning passed with nary a crow and we trudged back to the camp for lunch in a state of despair.

On our return to the bush we beheld a sight which produced both joy and dismay. In our absence the crows had discovered the owl. The limbs of the elm were covered with agitated black figures and the owl, which had been artfully hung to appear at rest on a branch, swung drunkenly in the breeze. Rooted in our tracks, we watched a crow launch himself from the topmost branch and plummet in a kamikaze dive at the owl, which terminated in a puff of brown feathers. As we rushed to the tree the crows departed hurling oaths over their sable shoulders and we were left with a demolished decoy.

This experience taught us two things: first, an owl does attract crows; second, it should never be left unattended!

The following spring we obtained another stuffed owl from Hector Bedard. This one had the refinement of both a reinforced hook in its head and a mounting bracket on the feet. The only episode worth recalling that year was a carefully planned shoot in a field at the edge of our property. This field had just been spread with fresh manure and clearly rated four stars in the crows "Guide Michelin."

Immediately after breakfast, on a crisp Easter morning, we set off down the road laden like pack mules. Our gear included the owl, fixed to a six-foot cedar post, and at least 300 shells. We meant business! Arriving at the field, we disturbed a good number of feeding birds and quickly planted the owl on his post. Our decoy stood out beautifully on a slight rise of ground, and could be seen from all sides. Scurrying into the blind we loaded our guns, opened fresh boxes of shells (to save time when the action became hectic) and waited tensely.

A word on our blind. The field had, in its center, a single large pine tree with boughs that nearly swept the ground. By moving in to the trunk of the tree we were completely hidden from sharp black eyes; a perfect natural blind. We were close to our work as well — the owl was only 20 yards away.

Soon after getting settled we heard excited caws.

Looking under the branches we saw a pair heading for the owl with a big gang following in their wake. As the crows swirled around the decoy we realized, to our horror, that we couldn't shoot. The low branches prevented any kind of gun swing or even a clear view! In desperation, we charged out of the blind, but the crows evaporated on the instant, and our shots found no mark.

Disconsolate, we plodded the long road home and resolved to give up crow shooting forever. While this did not happen, we never again occupied a blind that didn't permit a good swing at the quarry.

Recalling that incident reminds me that in those days our concept of a blind was a structure built along the lines of a fort. The walls had to be both thick and strong and, whenever possible, we added a solid roof. This approach is valid if one must withstand a mortar barrage, but quite wrong if the object is decoy shooting.

A good blind needs very little material. Its main purpose is to break the outline of the occupants. If you wear drab clothing and keep *still*, you can be invisible behind a few handfuls of grass or twigs. A sparse blind blends with the surroundings and allows you to watch and shoot approaching birds with ease.

When I was 14, Jack Heney's nephew Michael and I spent the month of August at the camp. Michael Heney was my age and a close companion over the years, particularly at Black Bay. He had a real feeling for the outdoors and loved the camp. We had a memorable time, with practically no supervision except when Dad came down for the weekend or an occasional week night. Our housekeeping and meals were looked after by the guardian's wife, Flora, so our only task was to keep ourselves amused. Which we did. We were on the go from dawn till dusk and the days flew by. In fact, we were described to Father as a pair of "river rats" by a neighbouring farmer, who meant the term as a compliment.

In previous years, wild rice had been planted to attract and hold migrating ducks in the ponds. That year, we had a bumper crop, but Dad observed ruefully that there would be scarcely a grain left by the opening of the duck season, as we had a virtual plague of blackbirds. Because of nesting ducks, shotgun shooting was forbidden anywhere near the marsh. Further, if we used a shotgun it was not to be fired at anything other than a crow. These rules chafed. Michael and I watched hordes of blackbirds flight each evening to the wild rice beds behind the camp.

During the first two weeks we speculated on the havoc we could wreak, but we kept our promise to Dad. Finally, one evening when the hour had passed to expect Dad, Michael took his uncle's Winchester down from the rack and said he was only going to fire one shot "to scare them away." Once out of the house he was joined by Barney, a liver and white spaniel, and they headed for the causeway. Standing at the window, I saw him stop opposite a huge flock. The birds were busily husking rice as they clung to the swaying stalks. Mike raised the gun and, at the report, a cloud of birds rose from the reeds, Barney plunged into the swamp, and Dad's car came round the corner. Dad had heard the shot, and pulling abreast, asked Michael for an explanation. It is just possible that Michael's quick wit could have saved the day if it hadn't been for Barney. Barney was not much of a retriever on ducks, and he was indifferent as a flushing dog on woodcock, but he had a strange passion for blackbirds. As Michael finished stammering his excuse, Barney clambered up the rocks and proudly dropped a very wet and very dead redwing between them. This feat was repeated four more times, and Michael's goose was cooked.

The next morning, after Dad left for the city, we took Barney back to the killing zone and made a thorough search of the area. The total that fell to that single charge was either 15 or 16, depending on whether you count a cowbird in the aggregate.

On a more positive note, during the same month we managed to keep Dad well supplied with fresh frogs' legs. In the process, we stumbled upon a novel form of shooting.

Prior to the raising of the Ottawa River, our section had a tremendous population of giant bullfrogs. Indeed, many local farm boys supplemented their meager earnings by the sale of frogs' legs to restaurants in Montreal, Hull and Ottawa. The eccepted method of obtaining frogs' legs was to pole a shallow draft boat along the water's edge at night, with a light and a spear. Normally, one man managed the boat and light, his companion the spear. In practice, the large twin orbs of the bullfrog caught the light, the beast was mesmerized by the beam, and shortly thereafter would be impaled on the trident. Many of the locals made their own spears by straightening three fishhooks and lashing them to an eight-foot pole.

This method was not for us. Being sportsmen, we decided to shoot our frogs, in daylight. At the outset I should warn that this procedure is fraught with hazard. First, the frog will frequently disappear as soon as he sees you. Second, the target is minute—a half-inch circle between his eyes. Third, assuming you hit the frog, he is likely to sink and never be recovered. We coped with the challenge in the following manner.

To avoid the danger of ricochets, we used .22 cap cartridges, which are practically silent and have low velocity, yet sufficient punch to slay a frog. Early in the game we learned the need for stealth and soon became adept as a pair of herons at stalking the margins of the marsh. Our shooting was excellent, but we found we were losing too many frogs because of their rapid sink rate. Pondering our losses, we had a bright idea — employ Dad's prize Labrador, Sandy, as a frog retriever. Sandy was dragooned into service and joined us, at heel, for the great test. In due course Michael shot a frog and I, in the capacity of handler, sent Sandy on a 20-foot retrieve. The dog plunged in, grabbed the frog, and started back to us. The picture remains with me. A beautiful yellow Lab, in his prime, moving with dignity through the reeds, a bullfrog in his mouth. Then to our dismay, the slimy prize slid slowly out of his mouth and back into the muddy water! We failed to take into account Sandy's tender mouth, so it was back to the drawing board.

Our final solution worked reasonably well. The drill was for the person not shooting to crouch in readiness by the "gun," and, at the crack of the rifle, to dash into the water and grab the frog with bare hands. Should anyone contemplate entering the frogs' legs business, I would suggest the spear is more effective, but the rifle more fun.

This was the first evidence that I was steady to flush but not to shot.

In our part of Canada winter comes early. By the end of November the Ottawa River is frozen, and by Christmas the area is cloaked with two or three feet of snow. By then the wildfowl have all gone south and a stillness settles on Black Bay. However, there is one sport left—

fox hunting. Over the years we held a number of fox hunts, which always took place during the Christmas holidays.

The central figure in these expeditions was an Ontario game warden, Percy Hedlam who, like his hounds, loved to run a fox. The party usually consisted of Percy, Dad, my two brothers, and myself.

Depending on the snow conditions, we would either drive in from the highway or take a sleigh. The camp was not winterized but nevertheless quite snug, and our only inconvenience was the lack of running water. I still remember the icy shock as my bottom touched the seat in the outhouse.

Each day we would set forth on snowshoes right after breakfast, and stay out until late afternoon. We didn't kill many foxes, but enjoyed ourselves immensely, and there was always food for conversation around the roaring fire in the evening.

One incident remains vivid in my memory. The hounds started a fox on the Snellier and the trail led north to Dumouchel's Bush. The fox's circuit was expected to include the corner where the road left the Snellier, leading to the highway, and I was assigned this choice stand. On one side of the road was dense willow or buck brush, the other was open field. The hounds could be heard baying on the far side of the field and there was every expectation that the fox would soon break cover and follow the fenceline down to me. As I was very cold, I put my gun in the crook of my arm, and rubbed my mittens together to restore circulation, to ensure a supple trigger finger for the "moment critique."

Suddenly, I had the creepy feeling that someone was looking at me. Turning around very slowly, I found myself staring into the yellow eyes of a big red fox who was standing, with one forepaw raised, at the edge of the willows. With my mittens on, and the gun under my arm, I could do nothing. The fox was only 20 feet from me, but scarcely inches from the safety of the bush. Having read that you could mesmerize an animal, I decided to hypnotize the fox with a piercing gaze, while I eased the gun to my shoulder. Our eyes locked for a full ten seconds and, confident the spell was cast, I slowly moved one hand to confirm his state of paralysis.

In a flash, the fox turned and, with a flick of his magnificent brush, was gone! My bellow of rage shattered the icy stillness and was heard one-quarter mile away. So much for the superiority of man over animal.

Being very much a "country boy," it wasn't until I was 17 that I was introduced to competitive shooting. The occasion was the first Alan McMartin Invitational Tournament at the nearby Seigniory Club. Father didn't shoot skeet or have a gun, so Alan McMartin, the host, kindly lent me one of his Brownings. Having never shot a round of skeet my style was apalling, which prompted an old duck hunter from Montreal to observe rather drily to Dad "I can see your boy learned to shoot in the marsh." Among other things, I rode out birds, missed *all* the clays at station 8 and ended the round with a badly swollen jaw from the stock. Despite my incompetence and the problem of gunfit, I managed to chip (not smoke) enough birds to score 86. Ironically, though ranked in the beginner's class, I lost by one bird to a middle-aged matron who had shot skeet for years.

On balance, the tournament was fun, but the outing marked both the beginning and the end of my skeet shooting career.

Duck shooting with Dad was an educational experience, although we didn't realize at the time we were being taught.

The first thing we learned was to identify ducks in
flight. This took the form of a game, and from childhood
we kept a sharp lookout for wildfowl. When we iden-
tified a bird we were expected to qualify our judgment.
This made us aware of flight characteristics, silhouette,
and wingbeat; the three main ways of classifying a distant bird.

Knowing species will not only increase overall enjoyment, but under the "point system," can make a substantial difference in the legal limit. To assist you, there are a
number of excellent pocket guide books on the market.

Shooting a duck can be relatively straightforward or
exceedingly difficult. The determining factor is the position of the bird in the air when you pull the trigger. Dad
taught us the secret, which is not gunpointing, but
"shooting strategy." Shooting strategy is the ability to
estimate the flight pattern of the bird, determine where
you want to kill it, and be in a position to shoot just *before*
the bird arrives in the zone. To accomplish this successfully, you must be able to identify waterfowl at a distance
and know their flight characteristics.

For example, if you are in a shore blind and see a
whistler approaching, you might plan to shoot him in
front, on the first pass, as he may not decoy. Just before
he arrives, ease to your feet and put your gun in motion;
the result will be an unhurried crossing shot, striking the
bird amidships. If however, you wait until he is in the
killing zone, before swinging into action, you will be *too
late* and have to fling a charge at his departing stern, with
little hope of a clean kill.

Another example would be a pair of blacks quartering
in high; you can tell by their wing action whether they
are likely to decoy. If they seem interested, *don't* blaze
away on their first high swing — you would be lucky to
scratch one down. Instead, use shooting strategy; choose

an area in the sky and when they lower into it on their second or third pass you will stand a good chance of collecting *both*.

When shooting from a blind it's best to ease into position. Ideally, the first shot should be fired before the quarry is aware of any danger. To do this, practice smooth gunmounting from a kneeling or sitting position; if you prefer to stand try and *uncoil* rather than popping up like a jack in the box.

Remembering all the things Dad taught us, I would have to rate shooting strategy as one of the most important.

Circumstances over the years were such that my two brothers and I were rarely able to get down to Black Bay at the same time in the fall. Initially, this was due to being at separate boarding schools. Then, when we had all graduated, John departed for service in Korea. The last time we were all down at the camp with Dad was in November, 1954, and we had the club to ourselves for three days in the middle of the week. Ducks were plentiful, but I remember most strongly the spirit of companionship. We knew that Dad was not well, and planned to enter the hospital shortly, but his warmth and infectious sense of humor made the gathering a very happy one.

On December 14, 1954, Dad died of complications following surgery. Over the years he had instilled in us a love of the outdoors and, by personal example, set a standard of conduct for us to aim at.

In accordance with the charter of the Black Bay Duck Club, Father's equity was purchased by the surviving members. Our tie with the camp was severed and, in the future, we would visit as guests.

chapter 3

Ducks

For four years after Dad's death we were all too busy trying to establish our individual careers to devote any time to wildfowling. John, the eldest, chose to stay with the family business which was going through a period of crisis. This thankless task was rewarded seven years later when he assumed the presidency, and ran the firm during its most prosperous years. Both my brother Guthrie and I left the business; he to work in the far north, and I to take a Short Service Commission in the Airborne Infantry, with the Royal Canadian Regiment.

As in the two previous years, Jack Heney kindly invited us to use the camp for any two weekdays of our choice during the 1958 season. These annual shoots were the high point of our Fall, as it was the only time we used our shotguns, and the dates were chosen with great care. By this time, I was in the financial business in Montreal;

so the telephone wires hummed between John and me as we deliberated the optimum time. We finally settled on the third week in October, in the hope that we would meet the "Northern Flight."

The first day dawned overcast, with a chill east wind, and we wisely chose to go to the Horseshoe. It was a wonderful morning for ducks, but we botched numerous opportunities through poor teamwork and/or poor shooting. Even so, our bag was ten birds, including a brant goose. John noted the flight was "spotty" and our shooting was "bad." The latter was an understatement.

The next morning was dish calm, with a bright sun in a cloudless sky, and we opted to spend the day at Omer's Pond, which was a tree-lined slough. Despite the bluebird weather we shot four blacks and three mallards. The diary records this day, October 21, as "The worst duck shooting we have ever had." Fortunately, neither of us knew what *really* poor duck shooting was, but we were to become intimately familiar with the condition before our next visit to the camp.

On our second night, sitting around the fire, we discussed my possible return to Ottawa and made a commitment to each other that if this occurred, we would take up duck shooting as partners. By Christmas I was transferred to Ottawa and, once moved, decided I would make my permanent home in the city. In making this decision, cogent arguments were presented to my bride Sandrea, who was from Montreal, but no mention was made of the fact she was destined to become a "marsh widow."

John and I immediately set about the task of finding a place to shoot. The first area we visited was, quite naturally, the Lower Ottawa River, but, after checking a 20-mile stretch, found every foot to be posted. With time running out, and knowing the river to be a major flyway, we turned our attention upstream. In haste, we settled near Breckenridge, which was 15 miles above the city of Ottawa. Here the shoreline was indented with reedy bays and one available section looked quite promising. We named it the Cove.

The Cove was a shallow, crescent-shaped bay, flanked on either side by much larger bays. Beds of reeds ran out from shore, and one long patch of wild rice ran from east to west, 75 yards from the water's edge.

Permission to shoot, and access to the marsh, was granted by the owner of the property, Hewitt Bell, on the basis of a handshake. Hewitt had retired from gunning, but he told us tales of great black duck shooting at the Cove in years gone by. In his backyard was an ancient double-ended canvas duck boat, which he agreed to part with for $10. John, being more affluent than I, paid for it and set about the badly-needed task of restoration.

In short order the old canvas was stripped, crude but effective carpentry replaced rotted beams, and the boat was recovered with eight-ounce duck. Two coats of "dead grass" marine paint and a new rope completed the refurbishing. Our sea trial proved it watertight, maneuverable, and skittish, with a marked tendency to tip. We were delighted.

The next item on the agenda was a blind. Paying careful attention to the surrounding cover, one was fashioned of indigenous reeds woven into a length of chicken wire. This hoop of rushes was then anchored with stakes at the edge of the open water. It blended beautifully. As the water was ankle deep, we made shooting sticks by attaching a 6 x 10-inch platform of 1-inch plywood to a three-foot length of 2 x 4, which was pointed at the end. These were to be driven into the mud and act as our seats.

John and I used double guns. Mine was a Browning

Superposed; bored improved modified and full choke, which had been a 17th birthday present. John's was a beautiful English sidelock by Cogswell and Harrison, with 30-inch barrels bored full and *extra* full. John once airily described the boring, to a shotgun expert, as being "Tight as a bull's ass in fly time." Which was true. The pattern at 50 yards was about the size of a dinner plate.

To complete our rig we purchased eight papier mâché black duck decoys. This set up was a far cry from the Black Bay Duck Club but we were confident it would produce good shooting.

The temperature on Opening Morning, September 19, was 36°, and we could feel a gentle wind on our cheeks as we walked through the field to the marsh in the pre-dawn darkness.

We had difficulty locating our blind in the dim light, and when we did, it appeared to have moved offshore. The explanation soon became apparent — the blind had remained secure but the water had risen. Cursing our lack of foresight we waded gingerly out, laden with guns, seats, haversacks, and decoys. Once the decoys were placed, we scrutinized the blind and saw to our disgust that the rushes had collapsed, lowering the protective height. Instead of a jagged outline, the top had a straight, boxline silhouette. When we got inside the enclosure and unlimbered our cunningly fashioned shooting sticks, it was obvious the water was too deep to use them. Due to the reduced height of the blind, and the fact that we couldn't sit, the morning was spent in an arthritic stoop.

During the morning one small flock of blue-winged teal came within gunshot, and we killed two; this was our Opening Day bag. We didn't see many ducks in our bay, but heard a lot of shooting from both flanks. Yet there was one consolation, and it was the *sure* knowledge of great sport when the northern redlegs came down.

Before leaving the Opening, I should explain that the level of the Ottawa River fluctuates with the activity of power dams upriver. This lesson was learned that day and we always took this variable factor into consideration in the future. As to the collapse of our blind, there were two influences at work: first, the rushes should have been thoroughly dried rather than applied green; second, a blind of this type is vulnerable to weather and, if possible, should be stored under cover when not in use.

In the days and weeks that followed the Opening we virtually haunted the Cove and on each visit expected to be greeted by dark rafts of northern black ducks. After 22 trips to the Cove (and 17 hours the previous weekend) John writes in the Log: "Hewitt Bell says be tolerant and not downhearted, better days are ahead." John then adds in brackets: "I bloody well hope so!" Our despair can be more easily understood by counting the bag to date, which was two teal (shot on the Opening) and one hen pintail!

Hewitt was, however, right in a sense, but the better days he spoke of were to come at Black Bay, rather than the Cove. Fate relented and our two-day shoot in early November was something to remember.

Our first morning at Black Bay we went to No. 4 Pond. The sky was overcast, the wind light and the temperature 22°. Usually, when one entered this pond the surface would erupt with as many as 200 ducks, but on this morning there was skim of ice and not a bird was seen. From 7 to 10 A.M., a total of five blacks visited the pond, of which we shot four, including a double for me. Around 10:30, Fernand Legault, the guardian, came to get us and suggested we move to Chatelaine's Island.

Weighing the loss of precious time against the possibility
of better shooting, we decided to take a chance, and go.

Chatelaine's Island was in the middle of the Ottawa
River, at the east end of the Horseshoe Island. It was a
tiny triangle of land separated from the Horseshoe by a
shallow channel roughly 100 yards long and 40 yards
wide. On the boat trip from the camp to the island we
craned our necks to see if any birds were flying over the
Horseshoe, but none were spotted. Indeed, we had a
moment of hestitation as we stepped ashore, but Fern
was serenely confident; and I reassured myself that he
wouldn't deliberately mislead an old friend. Our doubts
were not eased as Fern threw some hay on a framework
of cedar boughs and rolled a log up to the unsightly mess
for us to sit on. Clearly, Chatelaine's, which we'd never
shot before, was not even good enough to merit a *proper*
blind. Once Fern had departed we sat glumly for half an
hour watching the feather decoys tug against a freshening southwest wind, which soon changed to light rain. It
was very depressing. To pass the time we fished out our
sandwiches, put the guns on the ground, and started our
lunch.

By the time we were into our second chicken sandwich
the rain had changed to snow, and the tops of the trees
on either side of the channel were swaying in a half gale.
Suddenly, a single black duck passed directly in front of
us with cupped wings and buttonhooked back over the
decoys. At the shot he folded and splashed into the
weeds on the far side of the channel. In that instant our
mood of gloom was dispelled, and we quickly readied
ourselves for the next visitor. Within minutes a pair of
blacks made the same abbreviated pass as the first one
and, as they approached the spread, met the same fate.
John and I could hardly believe our good fortune. Luckily
our shooting was equal to the occasion. Throughout the

afternoon, singles, pairs and small flocks sought refuge from the cracking wind by piling into our sheltered channel. These were the real northern birds with "hairy" buff heads contrasting with sooty plumage and bright orange feet. Singles were taken by turn and when a pair came each would shoot the bird on his side. It was what I call a "clean" shoot, the birds acted beautifully, there were no cripples and our teamwork was excellent. That afternoon stands as the finest duck shoot we have ever had.

When Fern picked us up, shortly after 3 P.M., we asked him how he knew the shooting would be so good. With a little smile, he told us the spot was being "groomed" for a V.I.P., who was to shoot there the following weekend, and he had checked it every day for the past two weeks.

The next day we went to Omer's Pond. During the night the wind had abated, so the birds were very wary as they circled and circled our cedar blind at the edge of the pond. To make matters worse, our shooting deteriorated, possibly due to fatigue but, more likely, we were returning to our normal form. However, late in the morning a little breeze started from the northeast and by 1 P.M. was blowing about 15 miles per hour. For the rest of the day the birds acted much better, our shooting improved, and we finished on a strong note, with a very nice bag.

A footnote (literally) to this outing, was that early in the morning John went over his boots retrieving a bird. His brother, who had manipulated him into attempting the retrieve, saved the situation by suggesting that duck muffs (hand warmers) be substituted for his wet boots. This was tried, and worked beautifully. Indeed, for the rest of the day John stood in the dry blind and gave his brother hand signals.

Looking back, this was the best two-day hunt we ever had at Black Bay. As I have mentioned, the birds, all blacks, with the exception of six mallards, were beautiful specimens. The best 12 were given to Hector Bedard, so that he could make us a set of feather decoys. The heaviest black duck of the dozen weighed four pounds two ounces, while several others nudged the four-pound mark!

Returning to the Cove was a terrible letdown after our heady experiences at Black Bay. Yet we persisted in our quest for the mythical Northern Flight, with no success. Offshore, we could see a few small rafts of ducks but they refused to have anything to do with our bay.

Finally, we decided that drastic measures were needed. When we went to the Cove on November 17th, we had on our shoulders, not a gun, but a 100-pound sack of corn. With considerable effort, we laid a golden highway leading from the extremities of the bay to a spot directly opposite our blind. Here the corn was so thick, a duck could have walked on it. While our nefarious intent was probably indefensible, the reader may judge us less harshly if he considers, up to that point, our total kill was six birds in *31* outings.

When we returned the following Saturday, armed for a bonanza shoot, we found that nature had intervened and the marsh was completely iced over.

The basic lesson we learned from our season at the Cove was that you can't make a silk purse out of a sow's ear. If an area doesn't normally attract ducks, even the most alluring set of decoys will not alter the situation. To quote our old friend and counselor, Hector Bedard "Go where the ducks want to go, not where *you* think they should go." As we stored our gear for the winter, we were already thinking about a new location for next year.

Throughout the winter we pored over topographical maps, and, in the spring, investigated numerous leads, no matter how tenuous, in our search for a good marsh. From our efforts emerged two prime possibilities. One was ten miles upstream from the Cove at Beechgrove, and the other was roughly eight miles below the Black Bay Duck Club. Of the two, our hottest prospect was the area known as Presqu'ile, downstream from Black Bay. While this was on the fringe of the "duck factory" it had provided good shooting in the past.

Our lead into the Presqu'ile situation was a friend of Father's, whom I shall call Georges. Georges was a burly but soft spoken detective in the predominantly French city of Hull, who subsequently rose to a very senior position in the city's police force. At the time, his hunting club was disbanding and it seemed natural for John and me to join forces with him to form a new club. The plan was that we would assume the property his old group had leased, and augment it with some very good adjoining shoreline. The adjacent property was owned by a man named Martineau, but was under lease to a hard-nosed individual I shall call Labonte. To illustrate the machinations and political intrigue to be expected in the acquisition of a marsh on the Lower Ottawa River, I quote directly from our Log:

> May 26—S.E.W. and J.R.W. lunched with Georges to form the "Petit Presqu'ile Duck Club." Discussed forthcoming strategy re: leasing Martineau's side of the bay.
> June 1—Georges to Presqu'ile—talked to Martineau, nothing concrete—says we must keep the pressure on.
> June 11—Georges to Presqu'ile—stopped at Plaisance to talk to the Parish Priest—the good father says he will put the screws on Martineau.

> June 15—Georges to Presqu'ile to see Martineau—
> most cooperative and friendly. Says if he can break
> Labonte's ten year lease the property is ours for $100
> annually. Will know later. Georges paid for our side
> of the marsh, so win, lose or draw, will shoot there
> next fall.
> July 11—Georges phoned—Labonte is going to sue
> him for defamation of character!

The last entry made it clear that we weren't going to
get the additional land we needed, and, as a result, our
plan to form the Petit Presqu'ile Duck Club was stillborn.
Georges did, however, extend an open invitation to
shoot his part of the marsh, and we took him at his
word.

Our second choice was a reedy inlet on the Upper
Ottawa River, opposite Mohr Island, near Beechgrove.

The inlet and a few surrounding acres were owned by
a delightful French Canadian whose name was Joe
Proulx. Joe was, by any standard, very poor, but he
managed to survive by working in Hull and literally
living off his land.

The day we met Joe he was skinning a muskrat, whose
pelt we learned would fetch 75 cents and whose carcass
was destined to grace the Proulx family dinner table. On
subsequent visits he always seemed to be preparing
something for the pot. One day, as we watched him skin
a raccoon, John asked him if there was *anything* he didn't
eat. Joe paused at his task, reflected a moment, then with
a twinkle in his eye answered "Jean, there are only two
things you can't eat; one is a fox; the other is your
mudder-in-law!"

Dear Joe, he was the soul of kindness. When he rented
us his marsh for $25, he threw in the use of his boat!

Joe's boat was something less than seaworthy, so we
went to see Octave Charbonneau, the boat builder in

Hull, and bought a 12-foot flat bottomed rowboat for $40. Octave was a huge man with a serious hearing problem and a token knowledge of English. Our shouted conversations produced some hilarious misunderstandings.

To complement our new craft we bought a second-hand and terribly ancient Johnson 3 horsepower motor for $25. Both motor and boat were given several coats of olive drab paint. In fact, every item of our equipment, including thermos bottles, was marsh color.

Opening Morning was warm and misty. We poled down the inlet to the little bay at the end and set up a camouflage net blind, garnished with local grass.

As the fog lightened, we heard the whistle of wings and three indistinct shapes hurtled by. Moments later, we heard splashes in our decoys and were just able to make out several swimming forms. When we stood up, three ducks rose from our spread, but before we could shoot, were lost in the mist. Presently, a little breeze could be noticed, and, as our visibility improved, we waited tensely for another opportunity. Two birds were seen coming through the trees and, seconds later, a pair of woodduck circled our decoys. We each got one, with the first barrel, so the day started on the right foot. A few minutes later another pair of woodduck visited our spot, and they too were gathered. To this point we had each killed 2 woodduck, which, under the Game Regulations, was the permissible daily limit. Therefore we could not shoot another woodduck and remain within the law. At least 20 more birds decoyed, but *every one* was a woodduck and, to give us credit, we held our fire.

Finally, it dawned that this was obviously a woodduck "hole" and if we wanted any more shooting we would have to move, which we did. Walking down the peninsula to the mouth of the inlet we stumbled upon one of

Joe's traps, in which a raccoon was caught by the leg. We stopped to release the poor creature, but this turned out to be a dicey business, and I nearly lost a finger in the process. Once at the mouth, we discovered a natural blind site which provided a panoramic view of the river, including Mohr Island. We heard surprisingly little shooting, and saw damn few ducks. Those we saw were out of range.

At 11 A.M. we picked up our decoys and spent the rest of the day in the car checking out a beaver pond, which proved barren and a waste of time.

For the rest of the Fall we alternated between Joe Proulx's and Georges' marsh at Presqu'ile. Neither produced any decent shooting but one incident at Presqu'ile bears mention.

The marsh at Presqu'ile is a channel running parallel to the Ottawa River. Our side was reached by driving down a long field which terminated at the water. The field, used for pasture, was composed of clay soil which became slippery with the autumn rains. Traction could be a problem on the drive up from the marsh.

The day in question was miserable, 36°, with a driving rain from the northeast. Having arrived at first light, we set up a curtain blind at the edge of the marsh, which blended perfectly with the surrounding grass. This curtain blind was made of an eight-foot strip of tan canvas, with grommets every two inches along the top and bottom. Sheafs of dried rushes had been attached by running twine through the grommets. When rolled up, it was portable, light, and could be staked in place with metal pickets in a matter of minutes.

Around 7:30, a pair of blacks made a wide circle of our set, then banked for another wary pass. We didn't think they would come in, so we fired a salvo when we judged them to be at their nearest point. Both birds fell; but one was a lively cripple, which landed in some reeds on the far shore. Thirty yards from the blind, covered with grass, was the duck boat we had bought from Hewitt Bell. Racing over, I launched the boat and started poling furiously across the channel. In the midst of a vigorous thrust, my hand slipped on the pole; the boat listed sharply, and I executed a belly flop into the icy water. Fortunately, it was only waist deep, so there was no danger, but I got thoroughly soaked, and the cripple escaped.

For the rest of the day I sat and shivered in my wet clothes. To make matters worse, we didn't get another shot, and when it came time to leave, the car got stuck, resulting in a tedious tramp to get M. Desjardins with his tractor. On balance, a typical day at Presqu'ile.

The first day of our annual shoot at Black Bay was Tuesday, November 1, and, like homing pigeons, we went straight to the Horseshoe. The temperature was a mild 40° with a light east wind and occasional spits of rain. Birds flew well during the morning and we enjoyed some great ringbill shooting, as well as blacks and mallards. Around 1 P.M. the wind dropped, and, as the rain changed to a steady drizzle, the flight came to a standstill.

Sitting hunched, eating our sodden sandwiches, the conversation turned to the recent press report of a vice-president of General Motors, who had accidentally been killed by an old friend while duck hunting. We discussed the subject at length, then fell silent. The rain continued to drum and I found it difficult to shake the tragedy from my thoughts. Some time later John spotted a flock of birds coming from his end, which were on a course that would bring them quartering over us. When they were 30 yards out we rose, and, at my first shot, a bird folded. At the report, the ducks flared over and past us in seconds. Pivoting, with my back to John, I swung on a second bird. At that moment, his gun roared in my ear, and I felt a sickening blow on my shoulder which knocked the gun out of my hands and pitched me forward into the protective cedar.

John's alarmed inquiry penetrated my numbed mind and I answered in a voice choked with pathos "You've shot me!" There was a pause, and he shrieked "You stupid bastard, look on the floor!"

There on the floor lay a drake mallard twitching its last. This was my first bird which had plummeted on a trajectory that culminated by hitting me on the back of the shoulder, just after I pivoted. I retrieved my gun, which was stuck muzzle down in the murky water beside the blind.

The following day we shot Baie Dubaie in a spanking west wind. The birds flew very well all morning, but ceased to trade around 1:30. Nevertheless, we had a grand time and ended with an excellent tally for the day.

The rest of the season was spent on the Upper Ottawa. Using our boat and cranky motor we made a number of exploratory jaunts to Mohr Island, which we decided to try to rent the following year. In addition, we set for whistlers off the mouth of Joe's inlet and the tip of Robinson's Point. These expeditions produced few shots and even fewer birds, but we came to regard the goldeneye with great respect and affection.

Our final shoot was on December 10, which is exceptionally late for the river to be open. The Log indicates the temperature was 5° with a strong north wind. We set up on the sandy beach of the main shore in front of a row of cottages and built a driftwood blind. The wind was a mixed blessing as it kept the main ice floe offshore, but pierced us to the bone. Because our boat was icebound at Joe's, we placed the decoys within wading distance of the shore. I remember how our legs iced up the moment we emerged from the water. Once set, the decoys needed constant attention to prevent a heavy ice buildup which caused them to heel over. This was cold work.

Around midday, I shot a hen whistler as she glided over the rig with wings set. Several hours later a cock whistler appeared headed for the same fate, but changed his mind at the last moment and landed well outside the spread. John then stalked the bird, which was not easy, as he had absolutely no cover. Each time the whistler dove John would move four or five paces and then crouch motionless. At my signal that the bird was down, he would resume. The moment of truth came when John's last dash permitted him to stand in the *middle* of the decoys, and, to his amazement, the whistler failed to surface! The bird had swum rapidly underwater and bobbed up *behind* John, between him and the shore! My yell alerted him to the problem, and the bird was dumped as it attempted a hasty departure. Back on shore, it proved an exceptionally fine specimen, and was subsequently taken to Hector Bedard for mounting.

The next day the thermometer registered −11° and, although we drove miles, we couldn't find any open water; the river was frozen from shore to shore, and the season was over.

During the next spring and summer we continued our efforts to find a better shooting area. To be certain we had somewhere to shoot we renewed our lease on the Inlet with Joe Proulx, and negotiated a similar unwritten agreement with Emile Brazeau, a butcher in Aylmer, for Mohr Island. To ensure that we could reach Mohr Island in all types of weather we commissioned a larger boat from Octave Charbonneau. This boat cost us $75 plus our old boat, was 16 feet long, broad of beam, with her bow decked in to provide a storage locker. Our 3 horsepower "kicker" was traded for a 13-year-old Johnson 10 horsepower, which proved to be as much of a swine to start in cold weather as the little one. The paint job was a crazy-quilt pattern of dun colors, after the fashion of a World War I battleship, excellent camouflage on land or water.

For the past two years we had heard tantalizing reports of prime duck shooting in the Upper Ottawa Valley, but were never able to track them down. With a flash of inspiration we decided to advertise, and chose as our medium the Shawville *Equity*. The *Equity* was a weekly newspaper which blanketed the Valley and was read by virtually every literate English-speaking resident. To permit us to assess the areas accurately, we sagely decided upon mid-August as the best time, as the ducks would be out of their moult. Accordingly, on August 17, the following 6 x 6-inch ad appeared on the back page of the *Equity;*

WANTED
2 Brothers wish to rent or buy
INLAND DUCK MARSH
OR
RIVER POINT
MUST BE PRIVATE
Phone Aylmer Collect Murray 45359 or Province 70955 or write to Duck Marsh c/o The *Equity*, Shawville.

We cleared our calendar for the next two weeks to allow time to check the deluge of replies. Notwithstanding the fine reputation of the *Equity*, the response was zero; we didn't receive a single offer.

On Labor Day we took the big boat and made a detailed inspection of Mohr Island with the aim of selecting the best blind site. Superficially, Mohr Island resembled the Horseshoe in that it was in the middle of the river and had a pond of sorts. There the similarity ended, as the pond was too small to attract a decent number of birds and the riverbed surrounding the island was sand, hence there was no vegetation. We eventually decided to locate on a small shoal, 50 yards off the eastern tip of the island.

The next weekend we returned with shovels, an axe, burlap, twine and paint. With great care we dug just deep enough to avoid the water table. Once the trench was complete, the gently sloping parapet was ringed with driftwood. The interior was then lined with burlap. The result, a low semi-pit blind, was virtually windproof. At the end of our labors it is reported in the Log that we had a delightful swim. "Delightful" is the operative word, and I wince at the memory. What made the swim so pleasant was the clean swift water and the smooth sand bottom — but is this the environment of a puddle duck?

Opening Day was a warm 64° with the temperature climbing to 79° by noon. Our blind was everything we had hoped it would be and our new feather decoys looked superb. Because it was a prolific year, there were ducks flying in every direction and inevitably, a number of strays came our way. By the time we picked up at 11 A.M., we had three blacks and one blue-winged teal. John recorded "We find the puddle ducks are not too fussy decoying to the shoal." This was a gross understatement, and for the rest of the season, we didn't shoot a *single* puddle duck at Mohr Island!

At this time we kept our boat on the main shore, in front of the cottages where we had shot whistlers the year before. This beach was chosen because it was the last area to freeze. To reach Mohr Island we had to cross half a mile of open water in the bay, round Robinson's Point and then run a diagonal course upriver for another half a mile. The highlight of the next weekend didn't concern shooting, but a navigation lesson.

Due to the unseasonable weather the river was blanketed in fog, and visibility was less than 50 feet when we set out. Running at half throttle, we carefully crossed the bay, rounded the point, and headed, by dead reckoning, for the shoal. Both of us watched anxiously for "dead heads" as the river was strewn with them, and a collision meant, at the very least, a sheared pin. We had several narrow escapes, but after what seemed like hours, the shore loomed in front of the bow. We congratulated ourselves on a feat of superior seamanship. Our elation was short-lived. We had described a huge circle — the landfall was not the shoal, but a piece of sand 100 feet from our launching point! A compass became part of our equipment thereafter.

During the following weeks we substituted 24 plastic bluebill decoys for our set of 12 feathered blacks at the shoal. The nearest we came to success was when a flock of bluebills decoyed, and landed in the blacks. We happened to be jogging down the shoreline to warm up, and our guns were safely in the blind. However, we had noticed a fair number of whistlers trading steadily off the west end of the island. The only way we could figure to get them would be to change our boat into a floating blind and anchor it in the shallows off the island. This was the first time we tried to accommodate the ducks, rather than have them accommodate us. We resolved to mount an attack on the whistlers when we returned from Black Bay.

October 31, 1961, was the last time we were to shoot

the Horseshoe, and while we were not maudlin, we were aware that the end of an era was at hand. Looking around the pond, my glance was arrested by the majestic twin elms standing in the southeast corner. Invariably, if ducks were seen coming through the gap we knew their flight was destined to end over our decoys. By the next autumn these trees, and the others surrounding them, would fall. That day we saw only one flock of ringbills, but shot seven blacks and four mallards. When we picked up at dusk there was an extraordinarily heavy flight of hooded mergansers; perhaps they knew what was to come.

For the balance of the Fall we concentrated on whistlers off Mohr Island. Our boat was rigged with a framework of 2 x 4's to which we attached a Rolarush blind. The Rolarush was a type of curtain blind made of chicken wire through which long strips of reinforced paper had been woven. As the name implies, it could be rolled up when not in use. We used two curtains, one on each side, fastened bow and stern. To lower the silhouette and reduce the exposed opening, we lashed the curtains so they sloped inwards from the water level.

Arriving at our spot off Mohr Island, we would drive a picket into the sand, and run a line from the stern to a ring at the top of the post. This anchored the boat precisely, and permitted a speedy retrieve with minimum interruption of our shooting time. Two dozen bluebills were set on one side of the boat and five whistlers, in line, were placed on the other side. The curtains were then unrolled and lashed in place. As these were all-day excursions, we cooked our lunch amidships on a small propane stove which was stored with the food and utensils in the bow locker.

Our bags were never large, but we had a hell of a lot of fun, and kept at it until the end of November. On our last outing, December 2, we sheared a pin coming home through the ice. By the next weekend the river was frozen.

During the winter, Joe Proulx and his entire family perished in a flash fire which gutted their wood frame house one cold January night.

The fall of 1962 marked a significant change in our duck shooting fortunes. We finally got a spot on the Lower Ottawa. Jack Heney gave us the exclusive use of a 50-acre parcel of land surrounding Baie Dubaie, an inlet of the Ottawa River. Baie Dubaie was located at the extreme eastern boundary of the Black Bay Duck Club property. Before the trees were destroyed and ground leveled, it had been a wonderful spot for both bluebills and late season blacks. Now the section resembled a badly scarred battlefield intersected by a muddy channel, but it still held ducks.

Joe Legault, our helper, counselor and very good friend, lived adjacent to Baie Dubaie. Joe was a farmer, the head of large family, (Fern Legault was his nephew) and had worked for the Black Bay Club for years. Joe knew ducks. In addition, he was a highly respected figure in the surrounding countryside and something of a "swamp barrister." In fact, he was known as Le Petit Advocat, due to his short stature and authoritative opinions, pronounced in a deep voice. We built an excellent grass blind on Baie Dubaie. Our plan was to drive down each morning, leave our car at Joe's, shoot until dark, then drive home to Ottawa the same night. As Joe's house was one mile from our blind, we arranged with Joe for his hired hand, Alcide, to transport us to and from the marsh on his tractor.

The only exception to this routine was the night before the Opening, which we spent as guests of Joe Legault.

After a pleasant evening reminiscing in his parlor, we were shown upstairs to a tiny bedroom which unfortunately only had one bed. As soon as we had said goodnight to Joe, I asked John if he wanted to flip a coin for who got the bed. Sensibly, he pointed out that there wasn't enough room for one of us to sleep on the floor and added that if we slept "head to feet" we would be quite comfortable. I countered by asking if he had ever slept in a single bed "head to feet," and was assured that he had done so, with my brother Guthrie in Calgary, and they had slept very soundly. What I wasn't told was they were both extremely "relaxed" from copious draughts of Western hospitality at the Calgary Stampede.

Despite the lack of sleep we had a grand Opening shoot at Baie Dubaie, and this was repeated the following week-end. We were seeing lots of ducks, but more important, we were getting limit shoots every time out. John noted in the Log "We have shot more ducks in these first two weekends than we did all last fall!"

Our grass blind had been left out, and was by this time showing severe wear. Joe Legault built a cedar blind on the shore, which worked very well, but attracted the attention of some poachers who, from the number of spent shells, must have had a great shoot in our absence! To foil the poachers, we moved the blind 200 yards down the channel, to a spot which never attracted birds. The rationale of this move was that the poachers would use the blind, become discouraged, and eventually stop bothering us. Each weekend thereafter, we set up our portable rush curtain blind in the good spot. Our plan seemed to work.

One Saturday afternoon I crossed the channel to retrieve a cripple and, having topped the embankment, was amazed to see a steady flight of ducks trading between our property and Big Black Bay. The area they were using was a recently cleared section which had no cover or vegetation but was dotted with puddles. On impulse, I walked several hundred yards out on the barrens and knelt by one of the pools, to see how the ducks would react. Despite the absence of cover they flew right over, well within range. I didn't shoot but hurried back to tell John of my discovery. It took us a full ten seconds to decide to hunt there the next morning. The reason for this delay was that the property in question belonged to Stuart Molson, and clearly we would be poaching.

The next day was overcast, with a light drizzle blown on an east wind, and the temperature was a few degrees above freezing. For this operation our big boat, which was docked in front of Joe's house, was pressed back into service. Despite the cold, the motor started promptly and we proceeded down river at full throttle until we reached the mouth of Big Black Bay.

Wisely, the entrance to Stuart Molson's marsh was guarded by a barrier consisting of huge square timbers chained together to form a floating boom. Each length of timber had numerous steel spikes protruding from the wood; their function was to impale any boat that attempted to cross. Fortunately, there was a small patch of flat ground where the boom joined the shore and, with considerable effort, we dragged our boat across this beach to enter the bay. We then motored quietly down the shore, keeping a watchful eye for signs of activity at Molson's Camp, which was in full view half a mile across the water. The boat was beached where we estimated the flight had taken place the day before, and to confirm our judgment, we watched for five minutes to assess the pattern of movement.

Once satisfied, we moved off stealthily across the barrens with our guns in one hand and three feather decoys which were held in the other by their anchor lines slung over our shoulders. Thumping against our hips were the indispensable haversacks or "gunny bags" containing shells, lunch, and a pair of binoculars. We planned to make a day of it. Out on the flats we split up and I dropped my gear beside a living-room-sized puddle, while John continued 300 yards downwind to a similar spot. We placed our three decoys and knelt on the bare earth 20 yards or so back from the margin of the water. Our posture was reminiscent of a Moslem kneeling to Mecca, but our camouflage parkas, with the hoods pulled up, branded us as duck hunters.

We had not long to wait. Within minutes, three blacks altered their course and headed straight for my puddle with wings set. As they approached I kept my head down and remained motionless, but managed to sneak a glance at their blurred forms under the peak of my cap. When sufficient time had elapsed for them to reach the pond I straightened up from the waist and there they were, hanging in the freshening breeze, not 30 yards away! It took little talent to score with both barrels, but I was thrilled at the way the birds decoyed.

In the distance I spotted four specks working upwind on a course which, if maintained, would bring them within easy gunshot. Suddenly the ducks flared skyward, like exploding fireworks, but before their maneuver was complete one folded its wings and plunged towards the mud, followed by a second, which collapsed in mid-air. The muffled twin report of John's Cogswell reached my ears after the event.

Shortly after, I spotted another pair, but they had obviously seen John's decoys and were gliding in on cupped wings. The first bird never knew he was in danger and fell like a stone; the second rocketed straight up but was stopped in its ascent as though struck by lightning, it seemed to fall forever. Once again the muted reports rolled upwind.

Out of the corner of my eye I saw a pair swinging towards my puddle and quickly resumed the "Salaam" position. When I straightened up to shoot a pair of drake mallards were suspended over the decoys, so close they seemed as large as geese, and the green of their heads showed brilliantly against the somber sky. Candor forces me to confess that I missed *both* cleanly and watched stupefied as they paid off with the wind.

In retrospect, I am quite certain I lifted my head from the stock before pulling the trigger — a personal failing that has spared the life of many an otherwise doomed game bird!

The ducks continued to fly despite the thick wet snow that replaced the drizzle. Within a half an hour, however, the snow turned our decoys into white lumps and visibility was fast becoming a problem. John and I rendezvoused between our positions and decided to pick up and head back to the boat. This was not as easy as it sounds. Due to the driving snow, we had to use the wind to direct us back to the shore of Big Black Bay, which was invisible from the flats. On the plus side, the snow effectively screened our poaching activity and departure from the sharp eyes of Marcel, Stuart Molson's guardian. Having reached the water's edge it was a simple matter to follow the shoreline to our boat which had, by this time, a six-inch mantle of snow. On the way out we found we couldn't drag the boat around the boom due to the weight of the accumulated snow and were forced to clean if off with our bare hands. Once clear of the barrier we stuck close to the shore and made it back to Joe's dock without further incident.

The day had been tremendous fun and very educational. Previously, we had firmly believed the *only* way to hunt the canny black duck was from a properly constructed blind. This morning we learned that by crouching immobile, in camouflage clothing, one could get them to decoy like chickens, despite the complete absence of cover. This increased our scope in the future, and, from that day on, was known as "hunkering." It is of special merit late in the season when ducks are blind shy.

We should have felt guilty, I suppose, as we were both trespassers and poachers—these offenses could provide a court summons. Yet on the long drive home we were lighthearted, and our bag of ten birds was the more highly prized for being "forbidden fruit." Since then, there have been occasions when we have inadvertently trespassed while upland gunning, but that was the only time we deliberately poached.

The following Saturday, November 3, birds were scarce, and by mid-morning we had still not fired our guns. To relieve his boredom and restore circulation, John decided to make a tour of the property to see what he might flush. Inherently lazy and feeling that someone should "mind the store," I opted to stay in the blind. John returned an hour later with five birds; a pair of green-winged teal (on which he had doubled) two blacks, and a big bluebill. In his absence, the birds had started to move and I collected five blacks and a mallard. This was the total for the day and illustrates two home truths: first, in a good duck marsh you can usually stir up some shooting, if you are willing to walk; second, in the late season, ducks prefer to fly in the middle of the day rather than at dawn or dusk.

For several weeks we had observed a good bunch of bluebills rafting on the Ottawa opposite Baie Dubaie and the next day, Sunday, was devoted to a river shoot. Our big boat was loaded with bluebill and whistler decoys, the Rolarush blinds were stowed in the bow, and we headed downstream from Joe's to the junction of the Nation River.

The spot we chose was shallow enough for the decoy lines to hold, but too deep to secure the boat with a picket, as we did off Mohr Island. This problem was solved by an anchor arrangement that involved a locking pulley device with a rope that ran into the cockpit. The procedure was simple. To retrieve a duck, we pulled up the anchor until it clanged against the bow, and then motored slowly to the drop zone. The actual pick-up was made by reaching over the blind with the aid of a long-handled landing net.

That morning the temperature was 34° and, despite our parkas, the brisk west wind blew snow steadily into our faces. Our 24 bluebill decoys were set 50 yards down-wind. We strung five whistlers in line directly in front of the boat. The day was interesting, and we saw quite a few ducks, although we were disappointed to note that most of the bluebills had departed. Those that visited our set invariably streaked low over the blind from the east. As a result, the man at the stern would get one incoming shot but his partner, for reasons of safety, couldn't shoot. It finally dawned that the obvious answer was to move the boat *back* from the line of flight, to permit both of us a crossing shot. This might have worked, but we'll never know, as the bluebills tired of buzzing us and none were seen for the rest of the day.

During a quiet period, late that afternoon, John whispered "Mark left, your bird!" Grabbing my gun I looked quickly over my shoulder and saw that, for the thousandth time, I'd fallen for the old ploy hunters play on each other. The bird in question was a pigeon. A second glance revealed it was going to pass directly overhead and, as it was well up and moving smartly, it presented a challenging shot. At the appropriate time I raised my gun and swung through the bird, which folded like an umbrella, and whistled into the water 40 yards upstream. John merely grunted, but I felt quite pleased with the crisp execution. Presently the pigeon floated down to us and, as it came abreast, John scooped it up in the net. After examining it closely he held it aloft by one foot and said "Congratulations, you've just shot some poor bastard's prize pigeon." Sure enough, there was an inscribed band on its leg and I immediately had a vision of writing the owner:

> Dear Mr. Gauthier:
>   By now you must be wondering what has hap-
> pened to your lovely show pigeon (#HB756).
>   Well you see, we were out duck hunting and
> things were pretty quiet and . . .

However, I only wanted to close the incident. Accordingly, the pigeon received full honors and burial at sea.

We were contacted the next week-end by Fern Legault, with the exciting news that we could shoot Omer's Pond on Sunday. Omer's Pond, one of the club's best locations, was named after the owner, Omer Legault, Fern's father, and was rented each year with the stipulation that several days shooting be reserved for the lessor. Fern was kind enough to set aside one of those precious days for us.

Conditions on Sunday were excellent, with a strong northwest wind, but the birds were somewhat wary as the pond had been shot the day before. Nevertheless, we knocked down our limit of 12, all blacks. Only one incident marred an otherwise perfect morning.

This occurred when a wing-tipped bird came down at the end of the slough, roughly 200 yards from the blind.

Lacking a dog, I hurried to the scene of the fall. At this point, the pond was a morass of fallen alders which had been cleared from the bank during September. Fortunately, I had marked the bird precisely and within moments spotted a lively black swimming through the brush. At that instant, I could have shot the bird, but didn't have the stomach to desecrate its beauty with a charge of 6's at 20 feet. I decided to catch it by hand. Wading cautiously, I got to within five feet, and, looking the duck in its shiny black eye, made my lunge. A limb beneath the surface caught my foot, and acting as a lever, propelled me headfirst into the tangle, which quickly collapsed under my weight. With a loud "quack!" the duck skittered away and I was left spluttering and cursing in the icy water.

We never did get the duck, but it brought home to me the *necessity* of having a retriever.

During the Fall we kept in close touch with Joe Legault, who had a genuine concern for our welfare in the marsh. As the river started to freeze, it became obvious the end of the season was at hand. In the hope of getting one more good shoot, we turned to Joe for advice. He reflected on the problem, then instructed us to come back the following evening when he would have a solution.

The next evening we drove down to Joe's with keen anticipation and quickly learned that we were going to take a boat trip around Stapleton's Island. In the big boat were two 100-pound sacks of buckwheat.

The trip was an experience. The water surrounding Stapleton's Island didn't freeze until December, as it was both deep and very swift. In years gone by they had enjoyed great late-season shooting by baiting the adjacent shoreline. On this wintry night history was to repeat itself. In the inky dark our only illumination came from a small flashlight held by Joe, sitting in the bow. While John ran the motor, I sat amidships on the sacks of grain. For the next hour we were taught the nuances of "feeding" by an expert and perfectionist in the art. Time and again Joe's deep voice corrected our technique and directed us to put another handful "here" or cast it more sparsely "there." During the operation our boat pitched in the current and was frequently jarred by cakes of ice. On our way home we sheared a pin on an ice floe. With considerable relief we finally reached the dock.

The story has a just ending; when we came down Saturday to reap the reward of our illicit activity, the river was frozen solid. As two-time losers, our baiting activities were henceforth restricted to luring songbirds from our neighbor's feeders, rather than ducks to a blind. We weren't really disappointed however. The season had been excellent by any standard, and sensational when compared to the Cove or Mohr Island. John noted in the Log that on 17 trips to the marsh we had picked up an average of 7.5 ducks per outing and added "1962 was very good to us and if we never do worse than this, we will be very well off!"

The following months were ones of great change along the Ottawa River as large blocks of land underwent expropriation by the Province of Quebec. In February, we entered into negotiations with the Quebec Hydro Commission, the government body responsible for raising the river and subsequent expropriations. Our aim was to lease a 100-acre block, located between the Black Bay Duck Club holdings and Stuart Molson's property, which had been owned by Ovila Proulx, and, upon his death, leased by Molson from the estate. We knew that Ovila Proulx's estate had just signed the expropriation agreement and we hoped the new owner, Quebec Hydro, would lease it to us for a nominal fee, which they subsequently did. In the spring we received a renewable lease for a term of one year at an annual rent of $100.

We regarded the acquisition of Ovila Proulx's property, despite the short lease, as a significant step towards the realization of our dream to have a marsh in the "duck factory." Indeed, the location was perfect as we were sandwiched between the two best holdings on the Lower Ottawa.

Our section had no discernible boundary—the vegetation from Big Black Bay swept unbroken to the mouth of the Snellier. We established our territorial rights on a posting tour with the aid of our little duck boat. This exercise familiarized us with the marsh and brought home that the best way to hunt it would be from a floating box blind. Accordingly, we went to see Joe Legault, who agreed to build us one along classic lines.

The dimensions of the box were 6 x 4 feet with 12-inch sides and a 5-inch rim or gunwale. Metal rods were inserted at each end and in the middle, to form a super-structure for the dressing. These rods were bent to angle inward from bottom to top. A simple gate at one end completed the framework. With posts in place, two strips of 3-inch lathewood were wired lengthwise on each side, and the blind was ready for dressing (cedar or marsh grass.) The four outside corners had loops formed of metal strapping through which wooden pickets were driven into the mud to secure the rig. As the rings were larger than the pickets, the blind could float free if the water level changed, but the occupants were assured of a stable shooting platform. This blind was unobtrusive in size and perfect for two gunners. It was a joy and lasted for many years.

Just before the Opening, word reached us that our

lease was in jeopardy. An entry in the Log on September 5 reads:

> We are now embroiled in a fight to the death with Stuart Molson. He claims our lease from Hydro is illegal as Proulx's property was promised to him.

This caused us considerable anxiety, but our lease was confirmed, two weeks later, at a meeting in the Quebec Hydro offices in Montreal. The dispute was, however, the catalyst for a further change in our fortunes. On September 25, we became ex-officio members of the Molson Camp. To the union we brought the Proulx property as our dowry. Within a few days we consummated the marriage by moving across the bay, with all our equipment, to their site.

Molson's Camp was not as posh as the Black Bay Duck Club. The clubhouse, otherwise perfectly adequate, lacked a spare bedroom. The problem of our sleeping accommodation was solved by Stuart's partner, Hugh Garland, who rented us a tiny but comfortable trailer which we installed nearby.

Stuart Molson, whom we had envisioned as an ogre, turned out to be a very nice man with a delightful sense of humor. Despite a serious leg injury from World War I, he hunted with enthusiasm and was a crack shot.

Hugh Garland, some years younger than Stuart, possessed both great charm and an inexhaustible supply of energy. In addition to being a skeet shot of national renown, he was a keen hunter.

Life at the Molson Camp was very relaxed but, as newcomers, we were on our best behavior, anxious to convey the impression of responsible sportsmen. Through mischance, we shattered the illusion on our second weekend.

Upon our arrival Friday afternoon, Hugh told us there were quite a few Canada Geese in the Bay and suggested we try for them at first light. Shooting Canadas was a heady prospect, and it was well before dawn the next morning when we crossed the bay to our blind. As soon as our boat was secure in the cedars, we loaded our guns with high brass 2's and waited impatiently for sunup. Presently a pink light suffused the sky in the east and we saw numerous dark shapes hurry by overhead, but they were all ducks and we held our fire. Looking to the west, John saw a single bird coming head-on and low; its large size and deliberate wingbeat clearly indicated it was one of the Canadas.

We watched the bird bear down on us and, when it was 30 yards out, we stood up and plastered it with both barrels. The goose instantly crumpled under the hail of lead, and we exchanged hearty slaps of congratulations. Moments later Hugh Garland motored by in the half light and, in response to our jubilant hand signals, retrieved our goose. When he drew alongside, the bird was handed over without a word and we saw, to our mortification, the Canada was in fact a common loon.

The first year at Molson's was educational. Among other things, we were introduced to "push in" cedar blinds and Stuart's "sink-box."

The "push in" blind was a floating affair, with a base made by nailing two 16-foot lengths of telephone pole parallel, on a frame, so that they were roughly 4 feet apart. The topside of the poles were drilled so that small cedar trees could be inserted along their length. These cedars converged at one end to form a bow; the other end was left open to permit the entry of a 14-foot boat. The blind was held in position by an anchor attached to the bow.

When we first saw Molson's cedar blinds we were shocked. They looked as big as a house, and we were certain no sane black duck would venture within 100 yards. However, ducks reacted better to them than to our little box blind *with* our boat alongside.

The "sink-box," on the other hand, was practically invisible. It was used on the open bay, a body of water roughly two miles long and one mile wide. Originally, it had been a copper vat in the family brewery. Little more than a coat of paint, combined with some ingenuity, was required to change it into a superb gunning rig.

The main problem with the sink-box was getting it ready for use. First, we staked it in position, then filled the drum with a sufficient number of 50-pound steel plates to sink it so there was not more than 12 inches of freeboard. This was all hand labor and it took three of us to do the job!

With its low profile and flat grey camouflage, it was a deadly rig for bluebills as well as blacks. When in use, the sink-box required a boat to stand by as a tender, so we worked as a team and took turns shooting and tending.

One day when John and I were helping Hugh set the sink-box, we were regaled with a true story from some years earlier. Hugh had invited a rather elderly judge for the weekend and great pains were taken to ensure his stay would be a happy one. Friday night passed uneventfully, and early Saturday morning Hugh escorted the august personage across the bay to the sink-box. This location guaranteed good shooting, as there were masses of bluebills, and Hugh would act as the tender.

It was just getting light when they arrived at the drum. Hugh quickly helped his guest from the boat to the sink-box, handed him his gun and shoved off. Before Hugh had time to start the motor the stillness was shattered by a piercing scream followed by intermittent snarls and scrabbling sounds. In the half light the judge could be seen scrambling frantically to get out of the drum and Hugh hurried to his side. Once in the boat, the agitated man babbled of being attacked by wild animals. Within seconds, Hugh's flashlight revealed the source of his distress: two muskrats had fallen in the opening during the night. The judge left for Montreal within the hour, never to return.

We had good shooting that year and learned one very valuable lesson. A big blind with the boat *inside* is superior to a small blind with the boat *outside*. This may sound elementary, but it took most of the season to convince us of the fact. To rectify the problem, once again we turned to Joe Legault and he made us a miniature "push in" blind to fit our little boat. The following year it proved a great success and the foregoing observation was amended to read: a *small* "push in" blind is superior to a *large* "push in" blind.

During the next year, 1965, we continued to shoot in Big Black Bay on Saturdays, with excellent results. On Fridays, we preferred to "hunker" on the spit of land between Baie Dubaie and the Ottawa River which provided great sport, but also a challenge, as the section had been leveled and was bereft of cover. Looking through the Log, I see numerous good shoots. Friday, October 15, was typical.

The day was bright and the temperature an unseasonable 60°, relieved by a fairly good wind from the southwest. John and I arrived at Joe Legault's around 3 P.M., paid our respects to Joe, and sauntered out to Baie Dubaie. On the way we flushed only six snipe, which strongly suggested the flight hadn't come down from the north yet. By the time we reached the area we were to hunt, quite a few small flocks could be seen, trading back and forth. We watched them for a few minutes to discern the flight pattern, then separated, and took up positions roughly 100 yards apart. Between 4 P.M. and dusk there was a steady flight, and each of us got five ducks, one short of our limit. The bag consisted of six blacks and four mallards — most were "big northern birds." This experience gives one food for thought. We had no decoys, no blind and the surrounding terrain resembled a closely cropped pasture.

The key is to read the flight pattern. Most experienced wildfowlers will agree that ducks in a given set of circumstances will adhere to fairly rigid flight lines the way automobiles stick to the highway. If you imagine an invisible road in the air it is easier to visualize the pattern.

Once you know the flight line, your position must be carefully chosen to assure success. Camouflage clothing is important. Remaining motionless, with your head down, is *essential*.

As recently as last fall this knowledge stood me in good stead while hunting ducks on Wolfe Island. An old friend, Jimmy Williams, and I were deposited by our guide in a recently harvested 50-acre cornfield. Our rig consisted of eight silhouette goose decoys arranged in a clump, with no cover other than the six-inch high stubble. The guide departed shortly after we were set up, and for the rest of the afternoon we were on our own.

Half an hour passed with no activity, and then a flock of 50 ducks circled our field several times, but landed in an adjacent field. A few minutes later, a second flock followed the same air lane as the first. I noticed with both flocks that their corkscrew pattern brought them, on their lowest swing, over a point roughly 100 yards distant. Deciding to experiment, I moved to the spot. Shortly

after, I pressed face down in the stubble as another
bunch approached the field. This group obviously had
the same flight plan, and within moments they passed
directly over my head. I scored with both barrels. I called
to Jimmy to join me, which he did with some reluctance,
but his doubts were erased as a fourth flock zeroed in on
our position. For the next hour-and-a-half we enjoyed
some classic pass shooting, with a number of high birds
splitting when they thundered into the clay soil. Later in
the afternoon the wind changed slightly, causing the
ducks to adjust their pattern. We in turn altered our
positions.

By reading the flight line, and adjusting to it, we had a
great shoot. Had we stayed with the decoys, where the
guide had placed us, we wouldn't have fired our guns.

As ex-officio members of the Molson Camp, we were
fortunate to meet a number of interesting people from
Montreal, who came down as weekend guests of Stuart
and Hugh. One of these men, a veteran hunter, told us
at length of superb bluebill shooting on Lac St. Pierre
and, when pressed, gave us the name of a reputable
guide to contact. Fired with enthusiasm, we phoned
Pierreville that Sunday evening and arranged with Marcel Desmarais and his brother Gaston to guide us the
following Wednesday and Thursday.

Lac St. Pierre is not in fact a lake, but a widening of the
St. Lawrence River at a point roughly 30 miles below
Montreal. At the height of the fall migration it hosted at
least 50,000 diving ducks, mainly bluebills and whistlers.
A smaller river, the St. Francis, fed into Lac St. Pierre
from the south shore. I mention the St. Francis because,
one mile upstream from the St. Lawrence, its banks are
straddled by the village of Pierreville. The inhabitants of
Pierreville are commercial fishermen or hunting guides,

according to season, and the best known of them were the Desmarais.

It was still dark Wednesday morning when we pulled into the yard of Gaston Desmarais' frame house, perched on the east bank of the St. Francis. Introductions were made all around, and as soon as our gear was organized we descended the steep bank to the dock. John went in one boat with Gaston, and I went in the other with Marcel. With a minimum of fuss the boats were loaded, the big outboards started, and we glided swiftly down the St. Francis, its banks just discernible in the early light. When we left the shelter of the little river and entered the St. Lawrence a marked change occurred, and the boats bounced on the grey waves raised by a stiff east wind. We turned right at the mouth of the channel and ran downstream for 20 minutes, pausing to clear the propellers of floating weed, which had been torn from the bottom in clumps by feeding ducks. Our impatience was heightened by the sight of huge rafts of birds rising like smoke in front of us. We were greatly relieved when the engines were finally idled, and the two boats came together, at a point roughly one mile offshore. Gaston and Marcel, who had stood in the stern of their boats scanning the horizon during the voyage, had a brief discussion in French and then Gaston put his motor in gear and moved off. Marcel said we were going to rig out here, and immediately set about the task.

Both guides used 20-foot Vercheres boats, which are similar to a flat-bottomed rowboat, with modifications to suit the broad St. Lawrence. These boats possess a reputation for capacity and reliability. As if by magic, boxes of decoys appeared from under the seats, and we were swiftly fed over the side. Watching with interest, I saw that the decoys were attached at four-foot intervals by short lengths of codline, to a single heavy cord, which had an anchor at each end. The method used to place the decoys was to start by throwing one anchor overboard and then drift downstream as the rest of the string payed out. When the second anchor was reached, the boat was turned upstream, the bobbing line of blocks was towed into a U-shape, and the second anchor was heaved to secure the formation. The first horseshoe of decoys was reinforced by two more strings, and the last one was positioned to give the rig a pipe-shaped outline. To complete the spread, several pairs of whistlers were placed opposite the spot where our boat was to be positioned. Next, Marcel untied a long pole which had been lashed to the gunwale, and drove it into the mud bottom with vigorous thrusts. A rope fastened to the stern was hitched around the picket and our boat was secure. Once in place, the craft was camouflaged by hanging curtains of cedar branches along each side from bow to stern. These curtains were exceptionally compact for their length. They were made of very small twigs tied to a fine mesh gill net, and supported by slender wooden posts mounted in brackets on the gunwales. A cunning wire basket over the stern covered the motor, but permitted easy operation.

Shortly after we had loaded our guns, Marcel said "Regardez" and pointed to our downwind decoys. Seven bluebills were over the spread, but boring on towards us with cupped wings and dark paddles braking the air. I missed the leader with my first barrel and tumbled one of the tail end birds, a hen, with the second shot. Minutes later, another pair ran the gauntlet and I just managed to scratch one down. Marcel didn't shoot on either occasion and when I asked him, in convoluted French, why he hadn't fired, he told me that unless a big flock came he wouldn't shoot. Succumbing to my baser instincts I fervently hoped for small flocks.

There was a lull and then the silence was shattered by an incredible explosion from the direction of the shore; it was so loud the atmosphere seemed to crackle. Startled, I asked Marcel what had happened and he replied, with nonchalance, that it was just "Le Cannon." Further anxious questioning revealed that there was a National Defence Research Installation on shore, and they were test firing some sort of cannon. The firing range was the river, opposite the site, and we were precisely in the center of it! Each time the cannon roared during the next hour my hair stood on end, and it was difficult to enjoy the shooting. Around 9 A.M., a bright yellow cutter approached. As it drew alongside, we were ordered by the uniformed occupants to unload our guns. We complied, and then were interviewed by two R.C.M.P. officers who shook their heads when they saw Marcel, but questioned me closely. Finally, when they were satisfied I was not a spy, we were immediately ordered out of the area.

We lost time through this interruption, but eventually set up again three miles west of our original position. Bluebills visited this new location as did whistlers, scoters and bufflehead. The value of the picket and rope arrangement was illustrated several times when ducks landed in the main group of decoys, 60 yards downwind. When this happened, Marcel would untie the rope and we would drift silently down on the rig; invariably, we would get within 30 yards before the birds flushed.

Around mid-day the wind dropped, and, with the exception of the odd whistler, the ducks stopped flying. After an hour of inactivity I realized I was hungry and, quickly laying out my lunch on the seat, I started to eat. In the middle of a bite, Marcel ducked his head and pointing behind me whispered "Canard cheval," which is French for canvasback. I had never seen a canvasback, much less shot one, and there, flying across the smooth surface towards us, was a beautiful big drake.

It may be psychological, but I find birds are more difficult to hit in still air than when flying in a wind; further, the long crossing shot has always caused me the most grief. This bird had both in his favor, and to make matters worse, I wanted to possess it desperately, as this might be the only opportunity of the trip.

I watched the bird hold its course. When the gun came up, the barrels seemed awfully heavy and my swing was as creaky as a rusty gate, but the bird fell. I was delighted, and the lack of action for the rest of the day did not detract from this memorable event.

John and I had perfect weather the second day—spits of snow blown by a strong northwest wind. During the day we saw flocks of Canada geese, brant, old squaws and plover in addition to literally thousands of bluebills and whistlers. John told me the day before that his guide had used a "confidence decoy." I shot with Gaston the second day, and was intrigued by the beautifully carved flying bluebill which he attached to a slender pole and staked into the center of the rig. I had read of confidence decoys, but this was the first I'd ever seen.

Our two-day trip to Lac St. Pierre was everything we hoped it would be. The shooting was fun, and there was lots of it, as the daily limit per boat was 16 birds. From an educational point of view, we watched "real pros" in action and learned, among other things, to stay out of the cannon range.

Friday morning we left Pierreville and drove straight to Black Bay, arriving at 3 P.M., just in time to "hunker" on Baie Dubaie. The birds were flying well, and at dusk we picked up five blacks and four mallards. The following day fatigue finally caught up with us, and although there were lots of ducks, we were too tired to shoot properly, and wisely packed it up at noon.

The last shoot worth noting in 1965 took place on Baie Dubaie in mid-November, and we used our box blind, snugged tight to the bank. As all the shallow ponds were frozen, the birds were forced to trade between our bay and Big Black Bay, which resulted in steady traffic throughout the day. For a change, the ducks were decoying properly and we had some very nice shooting. I can still picture vividly a trio of mallards circling our rig with the ice blue sky as background. As expected, our bag consisted of blacks and mallards but we also had a blue-winged teal, which was most unusual that late in the season.

In November the afternoons grow short, and we should have picked up by 4 P.M. Instead, we chose to remain in the blind till dusk, hoping to get one more bird and fill our limit. When we finally set off in the big boat for Molson's Camp, we towed the box blind behind us as we knew a complete freeze could occur any day. By this time, it was dark and very cold, so John opened the throttle to speed us on our journey. The inevitable happened. The square end of the blind aquaplaned wildly, one corner of the box submerged, and the whole blind swamped. This necessitated a trip to shore followed by some heavy labor to dump and refloat the blind. Once we were shipshape, the towing operation was resumed at a more sedate pace.

When towing a blind or other bulky craft it is essential to go *slowly*. If the object in tow should swamp, or sink, your boat can be dragged down with it. For this reason, the tow rope should be held rather than tied, to permit instant release.

In our first decade we made a lot of mistakes, but also learned some valuable lessons.

The first thing is if you want good duck shooting you must seek out an area that *holds* a decent number of birds. This may sound elementary, but it took several years for us to accept the fact. Finding a locality that hosts a good population of waterfowl is only half the answer. The other half is to know how the birds behave in that region. Familiarize yourself with their feeding and resting areas, as well as their preferred flight lanes. These vary not only with the weather, but the time of day. The best way to gather this knowledge is to spend as much time as possible *before* the season observing the birds. If you can't reconnoiter the area before your hunt, then pick a likely spot, but be prepared to *move*. It is imperative to keep your eyes open and be mobile, so that you can go where the ducks want to go.

Many times we set up in what we considered was a great location and expected our decoys to pull the birds in—but it never worked. On the other hand, if you are where the ducks want to be, decoys are often unnecessary, and all you will need for a blind is your camouflage parka.

Countless other examples come to mind of ducks flighting in a peculiar manner, or working a seemingly uninviting piece of marsh.

On a recent spring day I was flying out of Kennedy for Montreal. Our plane was one of a continuous line taxiing down the runway before takeoff. Looking out the window, I was astounded to see a good flock of blacks and mallards contentedly dabbling in the flooded field less than 50 feet from the tarmac. As I watched, a small bunch came in from the sea and, setting their wings, glided straight into the pond. Considering the noise of the jets, it is hard to fathom why they would choose that particular spot, when there were hundreds of similar acres nearby—but that was where they wanted to go.

While it's not necessary to understand *why* they flight, it is *vital* to accommodate them, if you want good shooting. Our marsh has lots of ducks, but on most weekends we have to move one of our boats or blinds. A distance as short as 50 yards can make the difference between a limit shoot and a clean gun barrel.

In our early days we firmly believed that the more decoys you had, the better the shooting. Experience has taught us that this is only partly true.

Generally speaking, when setting for diving ducks the more the merrier—with one exception. That exception is the goldeneye or "whistler" —a relatively solitary bird, unlike his other deepwater cousins. The most effective rig for whistlers is two or three well-spaced pairs, or six in line. When hunting divers we always separate our bluebills and whistlers, placing the scaup downwind, and the goldeneye roughly opposite the blind.

Gunning for puddlers is a different matter, and we have found that six or eight *good* decoys are all that are necessary. These should be dropped in a loose formation, rather than a tight clump. When ducks are alarmed they draw together, but when they are relaxed or feeding they spread out. One or two decoys half-hidden in the weeds adds to the naturalness of the spread.

Our decoy rigs for divers and puddlers have one thing in common—a decoy placed exactly 40 yards from the blind. This acts as a marker to confirm when birds are in range.

Speaking of range reminds me that we used to shoot the heaviest loads we could get our hands on. The rationale was that magnum loads would permit us to kill ducks at fantastic distances, and compensate for aiming errors. Time has proved both assumptions false. The way to hit birds is to use a *balanced* charge and point the gun accurately. Nowadays, we prefer 1⅛ ounces of No. 6 shot and find it a killing load up to 40 yards—a very healthy distance!

Certain shots in duck shooting recur almost every time you're out: the low incomer, the decoying bird, the high overhead and the long crosser. Because I have missed them all, many times, I have spent a lot of effort in learning how to hit them.

Wildfowling calls for a smooth swing. The best way to ensure this is to imagine the bird has a vapor trail. I get the correct line by following up the "vapor trail" from behind, and the act of overtaking the duck causes me to swing freely. I would add a word of caution here, on birds you see from a distance. Don't start tracking them when they're out of range. This will cause you to dwell on your aim and stop your swing. Instead, keep your eyes on the bird, with your gun down. Just as it comes into range, mount your gun and fire *without hesitation*.

Low incoming birds should be shot well in front of the blind, so that the charge smacks them in the head and chest. If you let a low incomer get too close you will either destroy it completely, or miss clean and forfeit a chance for a second shot.

Decoying birds are easy, but here again, there is a right way and a wrong way to do it. The right way is to shoot the birds on the way in during their final descent. At this time their vital parts are exposed and the chances for a double are excellent. If you allow them to land and shoot them on the way out, you will be firing at their rumps, and the second bird will be at the edge of range. Both factors work against a clean kill.

The high overhead used to cause me great trouble but is now my favorite shot. Get the correct line by coming up the "vapor trail." Once on line, blot the bird out, pull the trigger, and *keep swinging!* If you do this you will be amazed at how easy it can be. The hazard on the overhead is stopping your gun once you've blotted the bird out. If you do, a miss is certain. The shot requires confidence, and it is essential that you pull the trigger at first aim — don't check to see if the bird is still there. It will be.

The long crosser is difficult for most of us, but once again I would suggest you get the line by tracking the bird from behind. On my good days I swing ahead the correct distance before pulling the trigger. On others, I fall into the common trap, and miss by failing to give enough lead.

One final suggestion. If you are lucky enough to have a bird come in very close (as sometimes happens in decoy shooting) keep your head *glued* to the stock. The great temptation is to lift your head, the better to view your quarry — if you do, you will miss. I know the problem well, and whenever I scratch on a particularly easy bird, this is usually the cause.

chapter 4

Geese

Geese are the aristocrats of the avian world and their presence in a marsh reduces other species of waterfowl to relative insignificance. Rare is the gunner whose pulse does not quicken at the sight and sound of these majestic birds.

The story of the greater snow goose stands as a testimonial to the vision of a dedicated group of sportsmen known as the Cap Tourmente Fish & Game Club. This exclusive club was comprised of influential men, largely of French extraction, from the city of Quebec. The club owned a long stretch of shoreline near St. Joachim and derived its name from a promontory high above the river, called Cap Tourmente.

Greater snow geese nest on Baffin Island and winter along the coasts of Maryland, Virginia, and North Carolina. At the turn of the century the only major stopping point on their spring and autumn migration was the area of lush tidal flats off St. Joachim.

By 1905, the population had dwindled to between 2,000 and 3,000 birds and the club, recognizing their dire predicament, voluntarily turned the property into a virtual sanctuary, with severely limited shooting. This pioneer conservation effort was rewarded, and the flock grew to an estimated 10,000 in 1937, 18,000 in 1940 and 40,000 by 1950.

As the geese multiplied, the club purchased adjoining land to accommodate their numbers, but eventually the private marsh could no longer support the total flock and a "spill-over" occurred. By the middle 1950's a pattern of movement had evolved, based on the availability of tuberous grasses, which could be classified into three general phases. The geese first stopped on the shoreline off Cap Tourmente. Once the meadows were plucked to bare mud they moved in loose flocks to the islands opposite St. Joachim, in the middle of the St. Lawrence. When these flats were denuded, they gravitated to the south shore near Montmagny. This was also the final staging area prior to the flight south.

The population explosion of the greater snow goose attracted hunters from all over the continent, and to accommodate them, outfitting establishments blossomed on both shores and L'Île aux Grues. As one might expect, the goose bonanza led to abuses and flagrant violations of the law. An overriding problem was the constant harassment of the flocks—airplanes by day and motorboats with jacklights by night. To relieve this deplorable situation, more game wardens were assigned to the district and, in the late 1960's, a long strip of shoreline near Montmagny and some of the offshore islands were declared sanctuaries.

Shortly after, the Cap Tourmente Club was expropriated by the Canadian Wildlife Service and turned into a controlled shooting reserve! Recently the flock was estimated at 85,000 geese. Had it not been for the concern and unselfishness of the club, today the species could be extinct.

My first goose hunt took place through the kindness of Hector Bedard, the year after Dad died. Hector and I read in the *Montreal Gazette* of excellent shooting for snow geese on L'Île aux Grues. With no firm reservations and scant knowledge of the situation, we blithely motored 300 miles to Montmagny one Friday late in October. Hector and I spent the night in Montmagny and crossed to L'Île aux Grues at 5:30 the following morning. The voyage was very rough and our small fishing boat pitched violently throughout the five-mile journey. At one point, the boat steadied and through the streaming window I saw a jiggling line of white blobs moving just above the angry waves. This was my first view of the greater snow goose.

As soon as we docked we engaged a truck to take us to L'Auberge des Dunes, owned by Gabriel Vezina, and were happy to learn on our arrival that he could accommodate us for three days. Within the hour we had unpacked our gear, eaten a quick breakfast, and were plodding across a mud flat (known locally as a "batture") which bordered the river.

Our objective, which we could see in the distance, was a low mound protruding from the shallow water of the receding tide. Once at the site, Henri, our guide, promptly set to work with a bucket to bail the flooded pit. His labor revealed a sturdy wooden box, roughly 7 x 3 feet, sunk flush in the mud. Its interior had a full length seat and a shelf for shells. In an astonishingly short time the pit was dry, and loose straw was spread on the seat

and around the parapet. Henri then moved 30 yards
upwind and proceeded to fashion a set of decoys with his
shovel by turning over sods and covering them with
white wax paper.

With three of us in the blind it was snug but not
uncomfortable, and the only drawback was the fine gray
mud which permeated everything. During the day we
saw numerous flocks trading up and down the channel,
but none came our way. A few singles did pass within
100 yards and each time Henri urged us to "shoot" (his
total English vocabulary) but was quickly vetoed by Hector. Over the years, I have found that many guides tell
their hunters to shoot at out-of-range birds; the rationale
may be that a hunter who fires a lot of shells will
attribute his lack of game to poor marksmanship.

The next day there was a brisk northwest wind and we
went to a pit far down the shore, opposite the church.
Despite ruined opportunities, due to indiscriminate
shooting from adjacent pits, we had several flocks decoy
and I learned a valuable lesson.

The first flock that came was a group of roughly 12
birds including seven or eight juveniles. The young can
be easily distinguished, as they are pale gray while the
adults are pure white with ebony wing tips. This particular flock had been flying along the waterline and, in
response to Henri's barking call, changed direction and
headed our way. As they approached, the wavering
string of birds reformed in "line abreast" and bore down
upon us with great purpose. When the guides' calls
blended with those of the geese and only the tips of their
broad wings moved, I knew they were in range. Pushing
off my safety I started up, but was restrained by Hector's
steely grip on my arm. Barely able to contain myself, I
watched the geese continue to lose altitude and grow
larger by the second. Finally, when I was on the verge of

nervous collapse, the moment arrived. The scene is somewhat hazy, but I have an impression of the flock sliding over us on motionless wings, and I can still hear their sharp cries. The sad truth is that I succumbed to "buck-fever" and, firing wildly, missed with both barrels!

Hector hit three with his magnum pump. Two splashed into the muck beside us, and a third sagged down in a long glide which ended in a cartwheel 200 yards distant. The guide trotted out to get the cripple, and while we were alone Hector cautioned me to pick a specific bird the next time and to keep swinging, as the speed of a goose was deceptive.

A few minutes later another flock turned our way and started their long approach. This time I waited them out and, to my delight, killed an adult bird with the second barrel. As this was my first goose, it was a prize of great interest. When I picked it up I noticed its thick neck and substantial weight, twice any duck I'd shot. The face of the goose had reddish brown markings, which Hector explained were rust stains caused by feeding in northern waters that had a high iron content.

In the afternoon the tide was far offshore and, during the long lull, our conversation turned to my error in judging the range of the first flock. Hector didn't labor the point but quietly noted the most common failing of the tyro was his inability to estimate the distance of approaching geese. His advice was "never shoot at a goose as long as it's getting closer." This is a bit of wisdom worth considering.

The third day of our stay was unseasonably warm and still, so neither of us fired our guns.

Our bag for the three days was small, but the trip was an interesting and educational experience. When we left the island I was a confirmed goose hunter.

Since then I have shot a great many geese, but I still

find their size deceptive. Estimating the range of these big birds is a common problem, and I have seen numerous hunters fire confidently at geese over 100 yards away.

If you have never shot geese before, or if judging effective range is difficult, I make one suggestion.

When geese approach, and you estimate them to be in range, hold your fire, and let them *continue in*. This shooting strategy assures close follow-up shots, if necessary. From the humanitarian point of view, it is far better to kill the bird instantly at 30 yards, than to cripple it at 50 yards.

Some people delight in trying very long shots, and when they connect it can be most impressive. However, when the gunner "misses" the bird is often, in fact, hit with several pellets, due to the spread of the pattern. Many of the pathetic, wasted cripples you encounter in the marsh are the result of long shots. Long shots *invariably* produce more cripples than dead birds.

Five years later John and I accepted an invitation from Leandre Roy to shoot geese on the Montmagny shore. Leandre ran a large textile mill in Montmagny and was originally a business acquaintance of John's, but this relationship quickly transcended commerce when each discovered the other's interest in goose shooting.

We stayed in a motel close to the river, and fell asleep the first night with the sound of 1000 geese in our ears as a huge flock fed on a nearby batture.

The next morning found us in a pit on the flats a few miles east of the town. Our set up was identical to those on L'Île aux Grues except for an ingenious difference in the decoys. Leandre's were made from strips of wax paper and didn't require the support of a clump of mud. Instead, each side of the paper was pressed into the mud to create a wind sock. As the windward opening was larger than the leeward, the paper remained inflated and resembled a lopsided Quonset hut. From a distance, they looked like feeding geese.

As it was early November, a good number of geese had already crossed the channel from L'Île aux Grues to our shore, which made Leandre optimistic. Some hours later we each had one goose, taken from the only flock to decoy, but by this time the tide was well out. As snows are inclined to follow the waterline, none came near us and the afternoon was a blank. Late in the day we were forced by the incoming tide to vacate our pit and set up on shore. Just before dusk a small flock decoyed and John and I got two more.

The final evening produced the most memorable experience of the trip. During the day the wind shifted to the southwest and Leandre said if it held, conditions would be perfect for a shore shoot at dusk on the high tide. This bolstered our morale throughout a long day which produced only one bird—a cripple that floated off with the ebb but was retrieved four hours later on the incoming tide.

By 5 P.M. we were in our new position on shore, the "papers" were out, the tide was mounting, but there wasn't a goose in sight. The minutes ticked by and the light slowly faded. Just at dusk, when the water was nibbling at our outermost decoys, the geese appeared. Looking far to the east I saw flock after flock, silhouetted against the pink sky, heading up the shore, and it reminded me of a giant flypast. By the time they reached us it was nearly dark and each formation announced its arrival with barking cries and then passed over us in line abreast. It was incredibly exciting in the half light with the roar of the surf blending with the noise of the wind and above them the high wild notes of geese. The

temptation to "flock shoot" was great and it took a con-
scious effort to concentrate on a specific bird. I picked a
single from two successive flocks, missed on the third, and
closed the evening with a clean double on the fourth.

As John and I walked across the fields to our car we
could still hear geese and, turning back to the river, we
saw a waving line of birds cross the harvest moon.

A few weeks before our visit the next fall, Leandre
phoned to say the goose situation was very bad — the
total flock was estimated at 35,000 compared to 65,000
the previous year. He recommended we cancel our trip
but, being optimists, we elected to go anyway.

A severe fluctuation in the snow goose population is
not uncommon, and usually occurs when the "hatch" is
destroyed by adverse weather. As the flock breed in a
fairly restricted area, this type of calamity affects the total
population. Nature fortunately intervenes to protect the
species by making the surviving adults much warier than
in normal years. Further, as juveniles invariably form the
highest percentage of the kill, hunting in an "off" year is
doubly difficult.

The first day Leandre joined us in the pit, even though
he knew our chance of getting a shot was remote. He
was right, but we enjoyed his company. On the second
day Leandre begged off as he had pressing work at the
mill, which left John and me on our own. Geese were
exceptionally scarce, and the main traffic along the
tideline was composed of eider ducks. By mid-afternoon,
we were bored and restless, so we took a walk along the
water's edge. Several hundred yards upriver we came
upon two local men crouched behind some boulders
hunting eiders. After a few minutes conversation it developed that they had some great Canada goose shooting
on a cousin's farm, well back from the river. Shamelessly,

John and I did our best to ingratiate ourselves, and we were invited to join them the following morning. Elated, we told Leandre of our good fortune that night at dinner, and were somewhat puzzled by his non-committal response.

Before dawn the next day we followed Claude's battered pickup truck into a farm lane, and then crossed several fields on foot until we came to a deep drainage ditch. We were asked to hide in the ditch while our friends went to get the decoys. Hurrying off to the truck, a final instruction was called to us, "Don't shoot until they land." As the sun came up we watched them stagger back carrying heavy crates. These were opened and to our dismay, out waddled seven Canada geese.

Our position was unpleasant as we were guests on the one hand, but on the other, we had no stomach to participate In a "pot shot" on Canadas lured by live decoys.

In a detached sort of way I was curious to see how the wariest of our geese would react to the "tollers" and yet, I hoped none would have the opportunity.

Fortunately, by 8 A.M. the geese had failed to show and, as our hosts had to get to work, the hunt was terminated. Possibly we should have taken them to task, but it wouldn't have changed anything. Instead, we chalked the whole thing up to experience.

The next year Leandre arranged for us to shoot with Joe Lachance. This was exciting news, as it meant we would explore the offshore islands from Joe's boat, and good shooting was a certainty.

Joe was a tall angular man, with hawklike features relieved by a ready smile. He was the eldest of seven brothers, all of them expert rivermen and outstanding guides. The Lachance family were born and raised on

L'Île au Canot, a tiny island west of L'Île aux Grues. Living in isolation, their lifestyle was rugged and their only link with the mainland was an open boat. Joe's accounts of their midwinter crossings of the seven-mile stretch were hair-raising.

Because of their background, the Lachance brothers gained national fame as consistent winners of the Quebec to Levis boat race. This race is unique as it takes place in March and the contestants, in eight-man canoes, are required to cross the St. Lawrence River during the spring "break-up." It takes expert teamwork and courage to negotiate the course, which includes hauling the boat across pan ice, pushing it with one leg over the side through floating slush, as well as paddling against the heavy current. Joe told us, quite matter of factly, that to get their boat to Quebec City for the race each year they would *row* the 50 miles *upstream* two days before.

We left Montmagny around 5 A.M. in Joe's small cruiser and headed straight across the St. Lawrence. There was a heavy sea and I remember a certain queasiness as we bucked our way through the dark waves.

After an hour Joe idled the engines and we rolled far offshore with no landmark in sight. The anchor was dropped and a small round-bottomed dory was lowered over the side. With considerable trepidation John and I gingerly boarded the small craft and Joe joined us, standing in the stern. It was still dark with a howling wind and, huddled close to the floor, I felt grave anxiety as we bounced over the waves. Fearing the worst, we resigned ourselves to a watery end. We were however, in expert hands and within minutes we beached on a tiny shoal recently exposed by the falling tide.

As the light increased we got our bearings and realized we were within five miles of the north shore; the high cliff we could see in the distance was Cap Tourmente.

Our shoal had a ridge which formed a natural blind, and a lawn-sized patch of flat ground for the decoys, which were a combination of "papers" and silhouettes.

When the first flock of geese were sighted, Joe hailed them with the "high ball" and they immediately swung our way. John and I knew we were listening to a caller of symphonic caliber and so did the geese, who came in as though on strings.

The shooting was very easy, and a refreshing change from the blank days of the year before. John and I both got doubles, and had our five bird limit by noon. At lunch we witnessed a calling demonstration on black ducks that was astounding. Three blacks were noticed pelting down the river at least 150 yards out from our position. We asked Joe if he could call them, which he did with a peculiar purring noise, and the birds made a right angle turn for our shoal as though they had hit a glass wall.

We took a lot of movies in the afternoon, and witnessed the arrival of three huge flocks of snows from the north, coming over Cap Tourmente. It was a spectacular sight and particularly thrilling when one realized that they had come all the way from Baffin Island to this precise spot. There was a mixture of triumph and weariness in their flight as they made the long descent to the lush battures of St. Joachim.

The next day Leandre, our host, joined us with two friends and we returned to the shoal. We killed a lot of geese, but the blind was crowded and, at the risk of being churlish, I must confess that I didn't like "gang" shooting.

After one particularly heavy volley John and I stood side by side in the blind and took movies of the carnage. I panned the scene and through the viewfinder was startled to see a supposedly dead goose right himself and

fly away. Dropping my camera, I grabbed the Browning
and shot the bird just before he got out of range. John, in
the meantime, continued to grind away with his camera.
The resulting footage is interesting, as you see my barrels
enter the picture, track the goose, and finally drop it.

On our last day Joe took John and me to the flats off
L'Île aux Grues. Using the small dory camouflaged with
cedars, we floated one of the tidal streams. Within the
first half hour we shot most of our limit and filled the rest
by noon. As geese are inclined to flight along the water
line, which changes constantly with the tide, this was a
clever way of coping with the problem, and indicated the
scope of Joe's expertise.

The afternoon was spent aboard Joe's cruiser. For the
first time we got to know him as an individual. Joe's
patience and clear pronunciation permitted us to cover a
wide range of topics in French. The trip had been exhausting because of the early morning departures and
this was a nice way to end it.

Fall, 1963, we were invited to shoot snow geese on
L'Île Marguerite. This small island near L'Île aux Grues,
next to L'Île au Canot, had been the birthplace of the
Lachance family and was now owned by a prominent
industrialist from Montreal.

The only structure on L'Île Marguerite was an old
farmhouse which had been renovated and now had a
large living room occupying most of the ground floor.
Directly in front of the house a stretch of marsh was kept
as a sanctuary for the geese; this provided guests with a
magnificent spectacle and ensured that a substantial
number of birds would stay on the island. Shooting was
done on the opposite side, from pits blasted out of the rock.

I believe that regardless of the location, it will improve
your shooting if you can set aside an area where birds

will not be disturbed. This is not only sound conservation, but also enlightened self-interest, as it will provide a reservoir of waterfowl to draw on. As the season progresses other birds will be driven into your marsh by shooting in the surrounding terrain.

We crossed from Montmagny in Jean-Marc Lachance's trim 25-foot cruiser, and were greeted on our arrival by his brother Alphonse, the guardian of L'Île Marguerite. After a quick cup of coffee we were driven in a specially fitted Land Rover to our pits across the island.

I was the first to be dropped off and Alphonse placed 12 full-bodied decoys in front of my pit before driving on with John. Conditions were perfect, with a strong northwest wind and a rising tide. Geese were everywhere. Minutes after Alphonse departed a pair came over, but I only smacked one. Shortly after, a family flock of four appeared to ignore my rig but eventually turned, well downwind, in response to my repeated calls. I crouched lower in the stone pit and continued to bark at them as they beat their way back, fighting the stiff wind. Having missed one of the previous easy pair I was determined to do better this time. As insurance, I held a pair of high brass No. 2's in my left hand to speed reloading, if necessary. On this occasion murder was in my heart. My plan was to shoot the two adults quickly, with the hope that the juveniles would linger at the scene long enough for me to reload. This is exactly what happened and although the second juvenile was a very long shot I managed to get the four of them.

Our next visit to L'Île Marguerite was plagued by hot, still weather. As the island was stocked with pheasants we should have hunted ringnecks. Instead, we stayed in our pits and got skunked for the first two days.

On the final morning we went to the eastern tip of the island and, as the sun came up, the geese started to move. For the next few hours we witnessed a truly amazing flight. At times the flocks stretched across the sky, numbering over 1000 birds. Unfortunately, we were just off the flight line, which was over the water, so the nearest geese were usually just out of gunshot. A few did however, stray within range, and we accounted for five before the flight dwindled.

At mid-morning we moved to the pits. In our new location I occupied the outermost trench while a friend, Herb Warren, was in toward shore. Birds were scarce, but an occasional single came by which permitted me to fill my limit. During this time Herb didn't get a shot, but declined to change positions with me. At lunch when we picked up I felt rather badly, but he very kindly said he had enjoyed the morning, just watching me shoot. This was as generous a compliment as I've ever received.

To this point our goose shooting had been restricted to hunting greater snows on the Lower St. Lawrence. However, we had heard of wonderful sport for blues, lesser snows and Canadas in James Bay. The next year we headed north to the Jack River on the east coast of James Bay.

When you look to the north on a map of Canada, you will note that James Bay is the southern extension of Hudsons Bay. While James Bay may look relatively small, its dimensions are impressive: 250 miles long, with an average width of 75 miles. Traditionally, all the geese who breed within several thousand square miles funnel down both coasts on their southern migration. Their final staging area is the mouth of the Harricanaw River emptying into Hannah Bay. Outfitters' camps are located along the route, usually at the mouth of a river which provides landing access for a float plane. Hunters normally reach the camps by chartering aircraft based at towns to the south, such as Val d'Or, Timmins, Matagami and La Sarre. It is worth remembering that this type of flying is dependent upon the weather, as the planes, operated by crack "bush" pilots, have few instruments. When planning a trip allow three to five days' grace as delays are the rule rather than the exception.

Our trip to the Jack River was a totally new experience.

On the first afternoon, the Cree Indian guides took us in a freight canoe (a broad beamed 25-foot craft capable of carrying prodigious loads) to the mouth of the river where it emptied into James Bay. The canoe was beached, and we walked two miles across the coastal meadow until we reached a small boggy pond. There, the guides built individual blinds for John, David Wright, and me by sticking willows into the soft ground. These small, circular blinds were set in a triangle around the pond. Fifty yards upwind, our decoys were formed by turning clumps of gray mud with a shovel. Several had a "nosegay" of white goose feathers stuck at one end, to mimic the white head of an adult blue goose. Viewed from a distance, the overall effect was most lifelike.

It was a sparkling day and the golden marsh grass which surrounded us rippled under a brisk wind. Within minutes a nice mixed flock of blues and snows was sighted. The guides crouched low in the grass calling with high-pitched cries. The flock came in with confidence strengthened by the low-throated gabbling sounds from the guides. My partners waited until the flock had entered the triangle before shooting and, in consequence, we all knocked birds down. Within an hour we all had our quota. The bag consisted of blues, snows and Canadas; a promising start to the hunt.

The triangular blind set is a deadly way to shoot decoying birds of all species, but most particularly geese. Three good shots sharing a single pit or blind will not kill

as many birds as three in one-man blinds. At least one of
the guns in a triangle will usually have an opportunity to
shoot, even if the birds are not "on line." On the other
hand, if the geese decoy properly, they will present a fair
target both on the way in and the *way out*. To reap the
full benefit of this arrangement it is imperative that you
hold your fire until the game is *within* the triangle.
Premature shooting in a triangular setup will ruin your
companions' chances—I know, as I have been guilty of
this misdemeanor on several occasions.

That night the temperature plummeted, but we were
quite snug in our sleeping bags in the unheated cabin.
Before we got up the next morning, a fire was roaring in
the stove which dispelled the chill from the air. Immediately after breakfast we set out in the freight canoe,
and hunted an area on the opposite side from the previous afternoon.

The last day of the trip was the only one of poor
shooting. The bluebird weather must have been the lull
before the storm, as we were "socked in" for the next
three days by a roaring nor'easter. This was particularly
frustrating as we didn't know when the plane might
come because the wireless transmitter was out of order
(as usual.)

These nor'easters usually last for several days, so Jock
Rushforth and I determined to do a little hunting. Our
companions objected, as they knew that when the plane
came in the pilot would insist on leaving immediately.
The flight time precluded an early arrival, so they agreed
to our shooting in the morning, provided we were back
in camp by 9 A.M.

Adhering to this strict schedule, we were just able to
reach the marsh, hunt for exactly one hour and then by
hurrying make it back by 9 A.M. The first two days no
birds came. The third morning appeared to be a repeat,

so we picked up ten minutes early. When we were half a mile from the pond the guide pointed back. Hovering over the empty blinds was a flock of geese. Behind them three more flocks could be seen heading for the pond. Had we waited those last ten minutes we would have probably shot our limit instead of being skunked. I suppose it was British Justice for leaving early, but by any standard it was a bitter pill! The plane came in that day at noon.

At the end of September the following year we went to the Pontax, 50 miles south of the Jack River. On the way in we lost a day to weather, and before we landed our pilot had to scan the rock-studded river to make sure the tide was high. This was a typical James Bay goose camp: a cluster of cabins on a tree-lined river, half a mile in from the Bay.

On the first day we trudged for several miles through soft muskeg to an unnamed stretch of salt meadow. In tribute to the energy-sapping terrain, we subsequently christened the area Cardiac Marsh. Despite the absence of wind, our efforts were handsomely rewarded and the three of us, John, David Wright, and I, had good shooting.

During the afternoon one heavily-hit bird glided out over the bay and fell dead 100 yards from shore. Anxious to see how my young Labrador, Shane, would cope with a goose in the water, I hurried with him to the edge. By this time, the goose was a motionless gray bundle floating on the placid surface. Initially, I sat Shane by my side and tried to give him hand signals. But he wouldn't go. After several abortive attempts it dawned that he didn't recognize the "lump" as a bird and therefore didn't know what to retrieve. To John and David's huge amusement, I picked the dog up in my arms and, carrying him like a baby, walked out in the water as far as I could go. Then, I pointed his nose at the goose and waved in its direction. This worked. Shane's ears perked with recognition, he started to squirm and when I lowered him into the water he took off like a motorboat. The retrieve started in unorthodox fashion, but finished in the most approved manner.

The second day we walked in on the opposite side but didn't have much success. Among some huge boulders, I did find a cache of Canada goose decoys, left by an Indian hunter for the next spring. These had bodies fashioned of driftwood which had been charred to give the proper dark tone, and heads from spruce roots, selected for their natural curve. The heads were also charred, and a piece of white rag had been glued on with porridge to indicate the cheek patch.

The last day we returned to Cardiac Marsh. This time the bay had angry whitecaps, kicked up by a howling wind. It was a wild day, and one of the first things we spotted was a large black wolf, who trotted away from us down the shore. The geese flew so beautifully that we found ourselves passing up shots or picking a particular species to prolong the hunt.

At one stage a large hawk circled our position. Stewart, the head guide, asked John to shoot it. However, as neither of us kill hawks on principle, John was reluctant, and asked why he wanted the bird shot. Stewart said he wanted to eat it, so John obliged, and later learned it was considered a delicacy by the Swampy Crees.

Stewart, like many of his race, regarded hunters' dogs with considerable suspicion. My Labrador was in particularly bad odor because of his habit of "keening" or whining when excited. Even though Shane's whines were ignored by the geese, Stewart continued to stare balefully at him. John told me after that, looking behind the Indian's dark eyes, he saw a vision of Shane's yellow hide gracing the wall of Stewart's lodge.

Fortunately, the dog redeemed himself with a courageous retrieve on a lively adult blue goose. The bird fell 30 yards on the other side of the breaking waves and Shane, new to surf, was bowled over as he entered the water. This happened twice more until he finally punched through the breakers, and caught the goose.

The Pontax provided great shooting but was essentially the same as the Jack River; this meant we still had more exploring to do.

At Christmas the following year I got in touch with an outfitter who had just opened a goose camp on the east coast of Hudson Bay, at Long Island. His sales pitch indicated that it was a veritable shotgunner's paradise with Canada geese as the principal quarry.

On the weekend after Labor Day we flew in an ancient DC-3 to the settlement of Great Whale and then took an equally venerable twin-engined Beechcraft 30 miles down the coast to Long Island.

Long Island was barren of trees or shrubs, but it did have a carpet of ankle-deep moss. It soon became obvious that game was scarce, as there were no blues or snows and only a handful of Canadas. The guides were sullen and uncommunicative. They did however take us for endless tramps across the moors in search of geese, which I didn't mind as the island had a haunting beauty. One gooseless day I watched an arctic fox hunt rodents; his success was little better than mine. In addition, we took several fishing trips to the Seal and No Name rivers on the mainland. Even the fishing was a disappointment. The trout were spawning and though they looked beautiful, they lacked fight.

On the last day John, Jimmy Williams and I arranged

to fly down the coast in the hope of finding some geese. We left at first light and after crossing to the mainland headed south. The pilot flew very low, which permitted us to scan the area with binoculars. Finally, at the mouth of the Roggan River, we spotted a huge concentration of Canadas. Landing appeared to be a problem because of the rocky shallows, but the pilot managed to take us down safely.

When we waded ashore we were pleased to find the treeless terrain was relieved by clumps of blueberry bushes. The two Indian guides announced they were going to shoot for themselves and, taking the silhouette decoys, promptly left us. Fortunately, there were so many birds trading back and forth that decoys or calls were unnecessary; all you had to do was pick a flight line and hunker in the blueberry bushes.

We split up and during the next hour had good but not easy shooting. My longest shot was a low crossing bird which I paced at 62 yards; had I realized the distance I wouldn't have fired. In the meantime we heard the guides shooting down the island and were surprised when they stopped, as the geese were still flying. Moments later they approached us and the reason became apparent; they had run out of ammunition. The law at that time permitted resident Indians unlimited shooting and a proposal was made to us that if we wished to pool our shells with them it would be permissible for us to continue shooting, provided all the geese we killed accrued to the Indians. The offer was attractive and, knowing the geese would not be wasted, we accepted.

For the rest of the morning we enjoyed superb pass shooting. Occasionally there was a lull but then we'd see a flock in the distance working towards us and the action would resume. As the day progressed the flight line drifted inland, which led us to a small bare hill surrounded by tidal flats. Crouching on the reverse slope we would peek cautiously over the crest when we heard geese and then retreat back down the hill when they approached. Flock after flock passed over this landmark. By noon we were running out of shells and Jimmy was reduced to using skeet loads in his full choked Remington. Fortunately, he was skillful enough to hit them in the head and the birds dropped as though poleaxed. To conserve ammunition and avoid cripples, John and I ended up firing only one shell, from our tight barrel, at each flock.

Early in the afternoon the guides rejoined us and seemed quite pleased with the results of our combined effort. As agreed, the Indians took all the geese, which was as it should be, but this caused us one small embarrassment — on our return to camp no one believed our story, as we didn't have a single goose!

That evening our party left Long Island for home, but only got as far as Great Whale. During the night fog rolled in from Hudson Bay and it was three days before we could take the DC-3 to Montreal.

Some years after the Long Island experience I went with Jimmy Williams to Winisk, on the western shore of Hudson Bay roughly opposite Great Whale. The camp was run by a white man but staffed entirely by Cree Indians. While the accommodation was indifferent, and the food only fair, the shooting was superb. Jimmy and I were assigned to the care of an Indian named Philip who, though he spoke no English, was a delightful companion and excellent guide. Hunting was done over countless acres of meadow which stretched in a broad band back from the shores of the bay.

On the first day we took Philip's canoe up the Winisk River and then walked inland for several miles. The area appeared to have little appeal for geese but Philip went about the task of building a willow blind with confidence. The decoys were fashioned by wedging goose wings in a stake, which was split at the top to receive them, and were most effective.

After an hour of inactivity Philip indicated we were going to move, which was accomplished with despatch. Our new location looked little different from the first, but it produced geese. Each time a bird fell it would be added to our decoys, with its head propped in position by a stick. By 3 P.M. we had a limit of geese which included Canadas, blues, snows and a pair of lesser Canadas, the latter about the size of Brant.

The next day we stayed on the mainland and were driven to our area in a surplus tracked vehicle. Again, the shooting was excellent, and by mid-morning we were taking pictures of flocks called in by Philip. One incident sticks in my mind. Just after daylight a small bunch of geese came over and two fell dead while a third detached itself from the flock on the way out, losing altitude rapidly. My Labrador, Shane, showing his experience, ignored the dead birds but took off like a rocket after the snow goose, whose trajectory indicated a touch down at least one-quarter mile away. The streaking buff dog and gliding white bird stood out perfectly against the stark background. When the goose hit the ground Shane was on him in an instant amidst a flapping of black-tipped wings. At the same moment Philip made a little exclamation. I sneaked a glance, and I saw he was grinning from ear to ear. The dog returned smartly with a good delivery and I wrung the bird's neck before handing it to Philip. It was only then that we found that Shane was the first retriever he'd ever seen. Several times during the trip I saw him shyly pat the dog, which endeared him to me, as Indians are not demonstrative in this way.

That afternoon we were treated to a new experience—
ptarmigan hunting. This was strenuous work as we had
to plow through the muskeg, but exciting sport.

In addition to geese and ptarmigan, Winisk had ducks,
sharptailed grouse and snipe. Truly a sportsman's smor-
gasbord!

Some years ago, after three unsuccessful tries, my
name was finally drawn for a two-day hunt at Cap
Tourmente. With precious permit in hand, Jimmy Williams and I drove down one day late in October. Our
attitude was one of dubious anticipation as we feared,
with the government in charge, the place would be
unrecognizable. Such was not the case. The Canadian
Wildlife Service has preserved the old clubhouse, unob-
trusively expanded the outbuildings to encompass research facilities, and maintained both the style and quality of shooting.

Prior to the daily draw for blind sites I lost both my
permit and hunting license, which provoked much mer-
riment from the bystanders, but caused Jimmy and me
considerable anxiety. Fortunately, we found them and
proceeded to draw our blind. Because of the tide, each
site had the use of three pits. The first was out at the low
water mark, the second was at half tide, and the third
was on shore, above the water line. Decoys were limited
to 12 tin silhouettes provided by the CWS.

The first afternoon we drew blind No. 9 and were
taken out to our pit in the time-honored manner, by
sleigh. While this is traditional, it is also practical, as the
deep soft mud is exhausting to walk in and impassable
for machines. The old reliable horse is just the answer.
Our pit was the same as all the others I had seen with
one exception—a watertight lid. This had a rubber seal
around the rim and a nautical locking device.

Geese were plentiful, but somewhat reluctant to decoy, so most of our shooting was at birds passing downwind with no intention of stopping. We were sharply reminded that geese can really move with the wind at their tails and had to swing freely to knock them down. Late in the afternoon the tide washed us off, but just before the pit flooded, Gaston took us to shore in the sleigh. We shot two more birds from the high water pit which made nine geese for the day, one short of our limit.

The next morning we occupied No. 1 blind but got blanked by a howling wind coming over Cap Tourmente which kept the geese offshore. It was however, very interesting and we were most impressed with the whole setup. With a little imagination you could pretend you were a guest, rather than the winner of a lottery!

Some geese, like some humans, are smarter than others. The expression "silly as a goose" may be valid *occasionally* with reference to lesser snow and blue geese, but it is grossly inaccurate when applied to Canada geese. Canadas are the wariest wildfowl I have hunted (black duck are a close second) and it is unusual to catch them off guard.

Goose decoys run the gamut from white paper plates to the skins of mounted specimens. Today, if I were buying decoys to use on land, I would choose the hollow-bodied shell type, made of plastic composition. These decoys come with detachable heads and, when ordering, it is wise to get a majority in the feeding or resting position, and only one or two upright heads to be used as sentinels for your "flock." Shell decoys are light to carry and, when disassembled, nest within each other compactly. Most important, they resemble geese, and quite definitely appeal to the big birds.

While I like plastic decoys on land, I still prefer the

traditional wooden decoys on the water. The way they "swim" and their sturdiness more than compensate for their bulk and weight.

When setting for geese, always try to place your decoys upwind. Geese like to approach against the wind and seem to focus their attention on objects to the sides and behind the spread, but largely ignore the foreground.

Most hunters believe that a large number of decoys is required to attract passing geese. To an extent, this is true. However, as few as 12 *good* decoys will frequently do the trick, provided of course, they are set in an area the geese are "working."

The most effective concealment is the pit blind. Unfortunately, it is also the most work. If you plan to shoot geese in the fields you can scratch the odd bird down by hunkering in drainage ditches or along fence lines. However, Canadas are wary and usually avoid these features. The pit blind is the logical answer. Many gunners drive countless miles on the back roads, stopping frequently to scan the grain fields with binoculars for signs of geese. This is an excellent way to locate a promising area to hunt the following day. I have only one word of caution: when you see birds in a field, don't disturb them—*wait* until they leave of their own accord. After they have departed (usually late in the afternoon) is the time to go in and dig your pits. Quite possibly you will have to dig in the dark, but by not disturbing them you will increase your chances immeasurably for a good shoot on the morrow. One last word, even if you know they don't come in the fields until 9 A.M. it is prudent to be in your pits well before that hour—sometimes they decide on an early breakfast.

Viewed from the blind, geese have quite different flight characteristics than their smaller cousins, ducks. Geese

take longer to come in and, once the shooting starts, are
slower to make their escape. However, don't be fooled
into thinking that they don't require lead. A goose
doesn't perform the aerial acrobatics that some puddle
ducks do at the sound of a gun, but they can move very
quickly indeed.

As geese often approach in flocks, it is essential to pick
a specific bird. If you don't, you are almost certain to
miss. The best way to hit geese consistently is with a
long, rather deliberate swing. It is one type of shooting
that lends itself to long-barreled heavy guns, as their
weight adds momentum to your swing. The goose is a
big tough bird which must be hit in the front end to
ensure a clean kill. When shooting geese I try to ignore
the body and concentrate on the head and neck as my
target. This is not unreasonable, as the head and neck
of a Canada or greater snow is equal to the total length of
most puddle ducks. The head and neck offers an excellent "tracking line," which is essential to the success of a
deliberate swing.

Turning to shotguns — automatic, pumps and double-
barreled weapons are all suitable for goose hunting.
Where mud is a constant factor, keep in mind that
automatics are very sensitive to grit, and hence are prone
to malfunction. The type of gun is not critical, nor for
that matter is the degree of choke, *providing* you shoot
your birds within 40 yards, and the shell delivers at least
1¼ ounces of shot. My choice has always been the
12-gauge, and I see no reason to change. In fact, I
consider the 12 the best all-round bore for wildfowling—
notwithstanding the cumbersome 10-gauge or the super
charged 20.

Over the years I have killed geese with all the shot
sizes from 7½ to BB. The sum of this experience leads me
to the conclusion that day in and day out, No. 2 shot is
the most effective.

When I think of geese, their size and stately bearing comes first to mind, but then I remember the extra something they possess — a wildness, echoed in their haunting call.

T.H.

chapter 5

Snipe

The Wilson's snipe is a grand game bird. His diminutive size and erratic flight make him a challenging target, while his clattering flush, accompanied by a piercing "SCAIP" can cause the most seasoned gunner's scalp to tingle.

John and I were introduced to "Gentleman Jack" many years ago while hunting snow geese at Montmagny. The marshy battures have always been host to migrating birds and we invariably flushed a number on our way to and from the pits. One fall, geese were particularly scarce, and we spent many tedious hours waiting for them. On impulse, one afternoon we decided to stretch our legs and investigate the snipe situation.

Holding our long-barreled goose guns at the ready, we set off across the muddy flat. Before long a snipe jumped and was missed by both of us. This happened 12 times until one ill-fated bird zigged when he should have zagged, which resulted in a collision with a charge of 2's. Fortunately, he was well out when the accident occurred and was relatively undamaged. We examined our trophy with great interest, concluding that he looked like an undernourished woodcock, but with longer wings. The bird was carefully tucked in a side pocket of John's parka and, fired with enthusiasm, we continued the hunt. Eventually I knocked one down and by the time we returned to the pit we had a total of four birds; one however, was a lesser yellowlegs.

The next morning we went out at dawn for geese but as the tide was ebbing, decided to quit at 9 A.M. John and I then raced back to the motel, shed our heavy parkas, loaded our pockets with high brass 4's and returned to the batture. As we had only seen snipe in the muddiest section of the flats we assumed this was their main habitat. We spent the rest of the morning slogging through the gumbo. We put several birds up but missed every one, and by lunch time were so exhausted we had to go home to bed. Around 3 P.M. we roused ourselves for another stagger through the mud. This proved more productive as we stayed closer to shore, where it was easier walking. By dusk we had fired nearly two boxes of shells and our bag was an impressive seven birds, including another error which turned out to be a golden plover.

The next morning we left for home, grateful to the little "twisters" for making our gooseless trip worthwhile. We had a lot to learn, but as we were thoroughly captivated with Wilson's snipe, it would be a pleasant task.

A footnote: I was plucking the snipe back home in Ottawa. Victoria, my eldest daughter who was then about four, burst into tears when she saw the birds and flew to her mother with the distressing news that Daddy had shot some baby ducks. The upshot was that I had to finish the job in the dark of our unheated garage with the temperature registering 20°.

The next year we shot geese with Joe Lachance on his boat, which didn't give us a chance to hunt snipe. We did get one morning shoot on the last day. Over the winter we had done some reading on the subject and absorbed two pieces of information: first, walk with the wind at your back, as the birds always jump into the breeze; second, use small shot. We large shot addicts viewed the latter recommendation with some suspicion, and we compromised by choosing 7½.

Our "beat" was a long strip of marsh running from Cap Ste. Ignace towards Montmagny. Its chief virtue was privacy. The day was cold with a scotch mist blown on a heavy east wind. Soon however, we were steaming with exertion. Two hundred yards of walking resulted in 12 shells being fired to no avail, as the snipe were wild. The next 300 yards depleted our ammunition severely with small return—two birds. Then we met the Giant Snipe. We flushed him twice going downwind at a cost of eight cartridges. The next time he rose we marveled at his size and, as he flew back over us, saw his shoulders were hunched with beak pointed to the ground (a flight posture we have since learned to recognize as "all business"). This time he lit near a willow bush which we marked as we hurriedly retraced our steps. To our horror we discovered we were out of shells! Thinking quickly, John said he would stand "guard" over the bird if I went for ammunition. John's guard duties were, in retrospect, somewhere between a warden and a washroom attendant. He loitered by the bush, while I raced back to the car. On my panting return we loaded our guns with trembling fingers and moved in for the kill. The bird flushed beautifully, but our salvo merely speeded his departure. Dumbfounded at our lack of success, we blamed the trap loads we were using, and tested to see if they had *shot* in them. By the end of the morning we had three birds, all Wilson's snipe, but I won't tell you how many shells we used.

In fairness, I will say that I have never seen snipe wilder, and we have dealt with cranky birds many times since.

As for the Giant Snipe, we remember him to this day, and wish him a long life with many progeny.

Opposite the city of Quebec lies a small island in the St. Lawrence, joined to the mainland by a long bridge; it's name is L'Île d'Orleans. Records going back 100 years confirm that this island and the Quebec shore have always been prime areas for the Wilson's snipe on his autumn migration. However, serious snipe hunters have dwindled in the last 30 years and only a handful remain who regard the "bécassine" as their favorite quarry.

The turning point in our snipe shooting fortunes came when we were introduced to two such men, Dr. Maurice Turcotte and de St. Denis MacDonald. These gentlemen had shot snipe since boyhood, and their regard for the bird was such that they rented a cabin on L'Île d'Orleans for the fall, so that they would be within easy walking distance of their beloved salt meadows. Maurice and Mac had little to gain from our acquaintance. In fact the reverse was true, as we were bound to put additional pressure on their "covers." Nevertheless, they generously took us in hand and, as a result, we not only made two good friends but learned a great deal.

The first outing with them was a revelation. They moved through the wet meadows with fluid grace, shot superbly, and seemed to find the downed birds without hesitation. Previously, we had understood that snipe were found only on mud flats, but soon learned that boggy fields and alder edges were preferred habitat. As novices, we had always walked the beat in a straight line. The advantage of a meandering course became obvious as I watched Maurice describe "figure eights" in a small stand of willows, and come out with three birds. The two "old pros" moved rather sedately but were never out of breath; initially we chafed at the pace, but soon realized this was the key to an all-day hunt.

During the previous winter both of us acquired open-bored upland guns; John's was a Webley side-by-side, mine a Browning O/U with 26-inch barrels, and our shells were standard No. 9 skeet loads.

At the outset we were very nervous shooting in the company of our instructors and missed some relatively easy opportunities. However, their good-natured banter soon settled us down and the birds started to fall. By the end of the day, we both had a limit of ten snipe and floated back to camp in a state of euphoria.

The next morning we went out on our own but did poorly. Most dishearteningly we lost three of the four birds we shot. Clearly we needed expert guidance to overcome our retrieval problem, so we stopped hunting and sought advice from Maurice and Mac.

We were told that the first thing you do when a snipe falls is to mark the precise spot, preferably by noting a bent blade of grass or some other irregularity in the foliage. Second, keep your eyes glued on the object and walk directly to it, ignoring any distractions along the way including flushed birds. Once the spot is reached, drop your hat and search the area in ever-widening circles. Further, when hunting with a partner it is the responsibility of *both* guns to take a line, so the point of intersection indicates the exact location of the fall. In this case, teamwork dictates who should fetch the bird, but under no circumstances should the stationary hunter take his eyes from the fall.

We took their advice to heart, and on the last day enjoyed an excellent snipe march, which was particularly satisfying as we only lost one bird of the 17 we knocked down.

The main snipe area on L'Île d'Orleans is a bench of flatland tucked beneath a high bank which runs along the north coast of the island. The terrain is mainly boggy meadows and damp pastures. Here and there one comes upon a field of alders or low willow bushes; both are ideal cover for the little twisters. Peculiar to the terrain are a large number of drainage ditches known locally as "rigolettes." These are a muddy nuisance to cross, particularly when the tide is high, as their depth can then be over your hip boots. To reach the flats a precipitous slope must be negotiated—easy on the way down, but exhausting on the way up. Fortunately, when you top the hill you usually come out into an orchard, and there is the prospect of an icy apple, plucked from the tree, as a restorative.

The following year when we returned to L'Île d'Orleans we spent the first day working a stretch from Gagnon's Rigolette to the old wharf. We covered approximately seven miles that morning and shot 12 snipe, which may sound like a lot, but works out to less than one bird per mile.

In the afternoon we walked a section of open marsh which ran east from the Quebec Bridge. The Log records that the birds were wild and it was all we could do to collect six. John notes that my new Browning Lightning 20-Gauge proved itself on a high bird.

The incident occurred when we were taking a rest and a stray snipe flew over us. It was so high we could just recognize it as a "bécassine." On impulse, I took one shot, leading the speck as though it were a passing duck. To the surpise of both of us, the bird crumpled, and pitched into a dense tangle on the other side of a fence. John shook his head sadly and said "You'll never find that one." Feeling that Lady Luck was on my side, I crossed the barbed wire and was delighted to spot its white belly as it lay in the brambles. Both the shot and the retrieve were a fluke, but nice to remember.

The next day a storm was brewing and we found the birds very skittish. We marched for miles on both sides of Gagnon's Rigolette, with a total for the outing of six snipe. Late in the afternoon the storm struck with a fury, and we found it very difficult to make our way back against the wind-driven rain. When we finally got home we were like a pair of drowned rats.

Speaking of rats reminds me of a shoot we once had at the Quebec Bridge. Our beat ended at the bridge and, as we neared the landmark, we noticed gray shapes scuttling amongst the boulders which form its base. Closer inspection revealed them to be giant sewer rats. We moved to within 30 yards of the stones and watched them dart in and out of the crevices. Not being above a little vermin control, John promptly smacked one with a load of 9's and I followed suit. We spent ten minutes at the scene and were amazed at their quickness, which demanded fast gunpointing. At the end of our brief hunt I was declared the winner, as I had dropped a big "buck" which must have weighed one pound and was at least one foot long.

Snipe enthusiasts, we were anxious to find some shooting closer to home as Quebec City was 300 long miles away. We explored a flooded section near the village of Papineauville and had fair shooting until the area was turned into a park by the provincial government.

Then we joined forces with Stuart Molson and Hugh

Garland in our duck shooting. The "merger" had an additional benefit—good snipe shooting on Baie Dubaie. In the first year we hunted snipe on the way to and from our duck blind with modest success. Turning the Log to October 17 I see where we got six snipe, in addition to a limit of ducks, which was typical. Later, Hugh Garland bought a small herd of cows which he pastured on the peninsula of Baie Dubaie with the express purpose of improving the habitat for Wilson's snipe. Hugh wisely restricted snipe shooting to specific dates, with excellent results. It was a great place to shoot. The cover was low and the ground was firm.

1966 was a good year and we spent three days, in late October, on the L'Île d'Orleans. On this trip we discovered a new "wrinkle" in our approach to snipe.

When hunting a tidal shore, the width of marsh varies with the height of the water. Over the years we noticed that at low tide snipe could be dispersed anywhere in the broad band of exposed grass. It suddenly dawned on us that the reverse must be true; at high tide the birds should be concentrated in the narrow strip above the waterline. Intrigued with the possibility, we tried out our theory on the last afternoon.

The stretch we chose for the experiment was a familiar beat which ran east for half a mile from the Quebec Bridge. We went upwind through the fields, well back from the shore so that we would not disturb our quarry. This circuitous walk was enlivened by the sight of two beautiful snowy owls, sitting on low haystacks, within 50 feet of us. Once upwind we could then make our march under optimum conditions with the wind at our back and a high tide.

When we judged the tide was nearly at the flood we set off. Walking parallel to each other, John covered the narrow band of open marsh while I winkled through the alders which lined the shore.

Our theory was correct and we flushed birds almost immediately. It was exciting shooting as the snipe darted and twisted through the alders like jet-propelled woodcock. John, in the open, was dropping birds with precision as they sprang from the grass in front of him, in addition to the odd one that I flushed, from his flank. Within 200 yards we had our legal quota and walked the rest of the beat with guns empty, in the crook of our arms.

It was a grand finale to the trip and this method is one we have used with good results ever since.

Another famous haunt of the Wilson's snipe is L'Île aux Grues, which most people think of in connection with the greater snow goose. The terrain is not unlike L'Île d'Orleans. The north shore is edged with mud flats and low meadows, while the opposite side is rocky. It is the only place, in our experience, where snipe can be so plentiful and lie so well that most of the challenge is eliminated from the sport. An English friend summarized his first visit to the island by saying "The snipe were jumping from the grass like mosquitoes!"

We have always gone to L'Île aux Grues for the opening of the season, the third week in September, rather than at peak migration time in mid-October. Stalking the battures in our bright clothing has caused comment from some of the duck hunters who also make a pilgrimage for the opening of the waterfowl season.

During a chat with an old school friend at a wedding in Montreal some years ago, the subject got around to duck shooting, and eventually to L'Île aux Grues. At one point he mentioned that on the previous Opening Day he had seen two lunatics trying to shoot ducks in the fields wearing yellow vests and hats. I didn't have the heart to tell him he was talking to one of those "nuts" and that the other was my brother.

On our goose trips to James Bay we always brought plenty of skeet loads, because it was wonderful snipe country. If you were in the right place during the migration, the shooting could be fabulous.

While at the Jack River I witnessed a most phenomenal snipe retrieve, which happened when we were hunting geese. It was a particularly slow day, so John decided to take a stroll and look for snipe. The area was a uniform sea of wheat-colored grass, with no distinguishing marks. John wandered off and eventually we heard him shoot a few times, well upwind of our position. After an interval, there was a single shot and we saw him go to the fall. A few minutes later he was still peering at the ground and, as he was bareheaded, it was obvious he had dropped his hat as a marker. In the meantime, our Cree guides had been lolling in the grass, apparently unaware of John's predicament. However, one eventually roused himself and ambled the 200 yards to John's position; once there he made a slight detour and, without breaking stride, bent over and picked up the dead snipe.

We had some nice shooting at the Pontax as well. One incident I remember occurred when John, David Wright, and I were shooting geese. Again it was bluebird weather and after lunch we dawdled by the fire with an extra cup of coffee. Suddenly, David pointed behind me and said "A pair of snipe just landed!" Galvanized into action, I grabbed my gun, loaded it with 9's, and started for the spot. As I hadn't seen them light, David kindly offered to direct me, which he proceeded to do with vigorous arm signals. Finally, when I was 150 yards out and had completed five large circles, it dawned on me that I had been "had." The Indians were still laughing when I got back; John and David were convulsed.

Quite a few years ago I was offered a trained Brittany Spaniel, and took the dog out for woodcock to test him.

Once in the alders the dog took off, and it was a full hour before we were reunited. Realizing that it was fruitless for us to continue, I decided to call it a day. On the way home we passed a favorite snipe marsh which I thought should be checked. Initially, the dog ran wild, but I ignored him and stuck to the task of putting up a snipe. At the first crack of my gun the Brit whirled in his tracks and raced to my side; within moments he had found the bird. Throughout the rest of the afternoon he stayed at heel and while he didn't point, he was a non-slip retriever. We had a delightful day and one of the highlights was a double, which I would not have attempted, had I not been sure the dog would retrieve both birds.

In retrospect, he was probably a very good dog; the problem of control could well have been my fault. At any rate he was a good companion in the snipe bog.

The only other dog I used for snipe was my Labrador, Shane. Our last outing was a three-day safari which I sold to brother John as a "Snipe Fiesta." The intent was to sample a number of famous beats on the St. Lawrence River below Montreal.

Unfortunately, it was a poor year for Gentleman Jack and although we marched miles of wonderful cover we had scant results. Included in the bill of fare were several islands near Sorel which were pastured by pigs and sheep in the summer. These islands had a reputation of being "sure fire" as the small hooves and distinctive droppings of the livestock made the terrain irresistible to the long bills. However, on this occasion they were very mediocre. We finally drove to Quebec City and spent our last day on L'Île d'Orleans, which was also a disappointment. Throughout the trip Shane behaved himself admirably, except for getting very muddy; this caused the interior of John's new car to both look and smell like a pigsty.

Some weeks later John reported that it had cost him a

fortune to get the upholstery cleaned and under *no* circumstances would he take a dog again. He hasn't.

One of the most memorable trips to L'Île aux Grues took place seven years ago. The shooting was superb but the journey to the island also deserves mention.

On this occasion, we flew in a tiny plane from Montmagny across the river to L'Île aux Grues. Our pilot was a delightful little man named Gilles, whom we liked instantly. However, we were a little distressed to learn, while over the gray St. Lawrence, that his plane was long overdue for a check-up. While we were digesting this disturbing news another small plane buzzed within 20 feet of us. Noticing our white knuckles, Gilles immediately took pains to reassure us and explained it was just his chum, who liked to play jokes. Once across the river our landing approach had to be aborted as there was a farmer's dog on the strip. The runway consisted of the backyards of four farms and was roughly 150 yards long, from fence to fence; the surface was, in the main, fallow potato field. When we eventually landed, after what one might describe as a "falling leaf" approach, John and I were most grateful to be safe on terra firma.

The following morning we were surprised at the scarcity of birds on the battures and adjacent pasture land. The few we did flush were wild and usually curved up to the high ground above the flats. By 11 A.M. we realized that something was wrong; their wildness could be accounted for by the east wind, but there should have been more snipe. Acting on a hunch, I suggested we try the high ground and abandon the damp lowlands. John agreed, without much enthusiasm, and we retraced our steps so that we would come out of the marsh near the church. On our way back I remember flushing a bird which I had to shoot quickly, as he was heading for sanctuary in the churchyard.

Once on the high ground we saw before us a long succession of narrow potato fields; these had been harvested and all that was left were bare rows of shale soil. To our amazement we moved birds immediately, and discovered the snipe were crouching in the lee of the furrows, to avoid the wind. When a bird flushed, the gale gave it superchargers and the result was that I missed more than I care to mention. John, on the other hand, was shooting beautifully. Finally, when we were into the third field, I got back on the "beam" and dropped a pair that jumped to my right and flashed past in front of me. A great advantage of shooting in the open fields was the ease of finding downed birds.

At the end of the stretch we came upon a small patch of alders which had been recently torn up by heavy machinery; a few trees were still standing, but it was mainly wet black earth. This three-acre plot held an incredible number of snipe and we estimated that close to 1000 birds departed on our arrival. We were so amazed that we didn't even shoot, but stood and watched them fly away.

The next day we returned to the potato fields and before we had finished walking the first field, noticed snipe flying overhead from the direction of the alder patch. To take advantage of the situation, we crouched by a fence line, and the result was that we had a marvelous shoot on "driven" snipe. The birds came over like feathered bullets and it took a fast swing to bring one down.

We found out later that a farmer had been working with his tractor near the alder patch and each time he made a circuit the noise would flush a number of snipe our way.

Hunting snipe requires a minimum of administrative preparation and little in the way of equipment. However, there are a few basic tenets to follow if you wish to obtain the most enjoyment and success from your shooting.

Water is the key to the environment of the Wilson's snipe. As much of their feeding is done by probing with their long bills, damp ground is a necessity. At times, they will lie up on high ground, but the constant factor in their habitat is moist soil. Ideal snipe cover is usually a combination of water, shoreline and low trees, such as alders or willows. The presence of cattle or pigs improves the terrain, as these animals pit the ground with their hooves, and their droppings promote a good crop of worms.

Once you have located a snipe area, it pays to check it frequently during the fall. Snipe are a migratory bird, with an autumn flight schedule somewhat similar to their upland cousin, the woodcock. Like woodcock coverts, snipe bogs can be bereft of birds one day but overflowing the next.

When flushed, snipe will usually head into the wind as soon as they leave the ground. Because of this characteristic, it is important to hunt them with the wind at your *back*. This way, the bird will jump towards you, and frequently present a nice crossing shot.

The terrain favored by snipe is, by definition, hard walking. The secret to avoid rapid fatigue (which also ruins gunpointing) is to walk *slowly*. At the start of the day it may seem unnecessary, but you will be thankful that you kept a sedate pace when the shadows lengthen. While marching for snipe it is best to assume an attitude of "relaxed alertness" as your quarry may erupt from the grass at any moment or, on the other hand, you may not see anything for half an hour. When walking in the open, I carry my gun pointed forward, almost parallel to the ground. Most birds will flush on a low plane and this permits me to get the muzzles on target quickly. When searching the alders, I adopt an upland carry, with the butt near my belt and barrels pointed at a 45° angle. Most snipe in this type of cover will tower to some extent before making a hasty departure. Therefore, the shot is likely to be at a rising mark.

Snipe shooting can be done successfully by oneself, but I think it is more pleasant (and more productive) with a companion. Ideally, the two guns should be 50 yards apart and abreast of each other. This way, any bird that jumps between you is in good range for one or the other, and each man has his flank as well. The effective "swath" of two guns is approximately 100 yards. On broad beats, with several belts of vegetation, including a border of alders, it helps in locating the birds if you separate, and one person checks the bushes, while the other stays in the open marsh. Once you have found where they are lying, you can regroup and comb the productive level in tandem. In this connection, we have noticed that snipe tend to lie "tight" on a sunny day, particularly if it was cold the previous night. High winds, or a pending change in the weather seem to make them wild, and under these conditions most will flush out of range—an exasperating predicament for the gunner.

Finding a downed snipe can be like searching for the proverbial needle in a haystack. Earlier in the chapter I mentioned the way we solved this problem, with both guns taking a precise bearing on the fall. Another solution is a well trained retriever, at heel. Lacking a dog, both guns should stop shooting when a bird is down and concentrate on recovering the quarry.

You do a lot of walking in search of the Wilson's snipe and proper footwear is essential. Hip boots, fitting close to the ankle, will permit you to negotiate the boggy ground favored by these birds. The rest of your clothing should be as light as possible, to the extent that you may be chilly at the start of the day. You will warm up after a few minutes of walking. A bright hat and/or vest is mandatory as the bird's sudden flush and irregular flight precipitates fast gun handling, which in turn can be hazardous to your partner. I know of one longtime snipe shooter who lost an eye to his companion's gun. John and I both wear bright hats and bright vests. When making a day of it we put a sandwich and a drink in the game pockets.

The most suitable gun for tramping the marsh is one that is light-weight and open-bored (improved cylinder or skeet). In past seasons we have used both 12's and 20's, but now favor the latter. The snipe is a tiny target demanding a dense pattern of small shot; regular No. 9 skeet loads fill this requirement perfectly.

Gentleman Jack is a good sport in that he often lets out a shrill "SCAIP" when he springs from the grass. This obliging trait will alert you if you haven't already seen the flush. I always enjoy his piercing call — even when he's out of range.

The most typical shots you will encounter are the straightaway, quartering away, and the sideslip. His flight is usually a series of zig-zags and I don't try and guess the next lap, but swing freely and pull as I pass his bill. Most snipe (like most woodcock) are missed by shooting too soon. I find it best to go after them without haste, using a full or slightly abbreviated swing. When a snipe jumps at your feet he will often scoot away low, just above the grass. In this case, I pause before mounting my gun to let him get out. It is important to get your cheek well down on the stock for this shot or your pattern will go over his head. When birds are in the alders they can jink through the branches with incredible speed and agility. In this type of cover a snap shot is the best (and only) solution.

On balance, snipe shooting is not as difficult as it is sometimes reported to be. Having said that, I am reminded of the last bird I shot at; he didn't bother to zig or zag but bored straightaway with his shoulders hunched and his bill pointed to the ground. It was dead easy, and I missed with both barrels.

chapter 6

Upland Birds

When I think of upland birds, two come to mind: ruffed grouse and the American woodcock.

Ruffed grouse is a grand game bird and an exciting adversary. He is canny, but his behavior is relatively consistent.

The American woodcock, on the other hand, is an enigma. His comings and goings are unpredictable, his habits capricious, and his flight erratic. Long ago I succumbed to the spell of this woodland snipe.

Good cover for woodcock and grouse, in my part of the country, means low poplar interspersed with birch and cedar. If you add hawthorn bushes and the occasional apple tree in the grassy openings, it is even better. To make it perfect, rim the stand with alders and a clump of dense conifers.

I was in my 'teens when I shot my first woodcock at

the Black Bay Duck Club. Since then, I have looked
forward to his autumnal visits and find I devote more
time each year in his pursuit. At the height of the
woodcock migration, my family and office are neglected
in favor of the russet twister.

My first significant experience with ruffed grouse took
place many years ago when a friend of the family invited
me up to his fishing camp for a day's partridge hunting.

We left Ottawa early in the morning so that we could
reach camp on the Upper Ottawa shortly after daylight.
Driving in the dirt road to the lodge, Bill stopped the car
suddenly when a grouse appeared in front of us. I was
given the nod and, opening the door quietly, stepped out
on the gravel and slipped a pair of 7½'s in my heavy
Browning.

The bird didn't flush, so I said "shoo!" It stayed rooted
to the spot and merely nodded at me. This happened
several times and then I heard the car door open and
footsteps behind me. There was a short pause before the
stillness of the morning was shattered by the roar of Bill's
gun and the partridge was sent kicking in the dust. I
immediately protested that if we'd been patient the bird
would have flown, but was told in no uncertain terms
that when you saw a grouse you shot it. I was surprised
at his attitude. Bill was a good wingshot, but it was clear
he regarded grouse as a crop to be harvested, rather than
a sporting bird.

We completed the journey to the camp in strained
silence and by mutual consent decided to hunt separately
for the morning, but meet at lunch. The car was parked
at the junction of two lumber trails which permitted us to
set off in oppostite directions.

It was a bright morning after a cold night, and I
flushed a good number of birds sunning themselves on

the path, but only hit one. When we compared notes at noon, my single "pat" caused Bill to raise his eyebrows. He had heard me shooting and expected more birds. In the afternoon I was sent down a bush road, which edged the lake, and missed a straightforward crossing bird before I had gone 100 yards. For the next mile I saw nothing.

By this time my thoughts were grim, but I was snapped from my reverie by the sight of a grouse which materialized 20 paces away on the verge of the road. Halting, I gripped my gun at the ready and yelled "shoo!" The grouse puffed himself up, fanned his tail, and with great dignity disappeared into the foliage. Shaken, I watched the spot intently and moments later my heart thumped as once again he cakewalked out on the gravel. Swiftly losing all semblance of control I croaked "shoo!" which prompted him to fix me with a haughty stare before he turned his back, and stepping daintily, evaporated into the bushes. By this time I was completely unstrung, but determined to bag the grouse by fair means or foul. Specifically, I decided that should the partridge reappear he would be greeted by 1⅛ ounces of chilled shot. Sure enough, he stalked out for one more curtain call. I leveled the gun, closed my eyes, and missed. The bird flew off through the shrubbery and I was left to contemplate both my squalid intent and gross incompetence. The experience was traumatic; it marked the last time I attempted to pot a grouse.

After that incident I slunk down the road and gradually slipped into a state of melancholia. This might well have been terminal if a pair of "pats" hadn't erupted from a clearing on my right. At the roar of their flush I swung on one which tumbled, and then swiftly covered the second, which also fell in a puff of feathers.

Stunned at the turn of events I was suddenly gripped

by a new fear; that I wouldn't find either. The area in which they dropped was a multi-colored carpet of leaves and neither bird was visible at first glance. Hunting frantically, I found one and then moments later let out a war whoop as I spotted the other. It is axiomatic that grouse hunters subject to both elation and despair.

On the way back, I got one more grouse as it jumped at my feet and flew straight down the avenue of trees. This completed my shooting for the day.

The outing was not a success in one respect, as my friendship with Bill hasn't been the same since. However, it provided my first double on "partridge" and helped to establish a grouse-shooting ethic for the future.

My upland gunning took a dramatic turn for the better when I linked up with Len Baillie. Len might be described as a natural gentleman; he is inherently nice and a great partner in the bush. Among his personal attributes is the ability to train and handle pointing dogs; he can also handle his 20-gauge. Len brought to our shooting partnership a fine German Shorthair named Barney, and the three of us shared many wonderful days afield.

Unfortunately, business prompted Len to move away, and I subsequently learned that Barney succumbed to wounds incurred in a dog fight. Leafing through my notes, I come upon various incidents from over the years, and while none are of great import, they may be of interest.

Len was a long-time grouse hunter and in consequence, placed "old ruff" at the top of his list, while I was inclined to favor the timberdoodle. This caused a good natured tug-of-war over the years as to which type of cover we would hunt. When I first met Len he had a "string" of fine grouse bushes, but none that were especially attractive to woodcock. To right this imbalance, we set about "prospecting" and soon learned that dense alders were not necessarily the best habitat for the long-bills. Because our woodcock season is short we would hunt them from Opening Day on, and found that in hot weather scenting conditions would deteriorate in the heat of the day, but improve as it cooled in the late afternoon. Eventually we accumulated a nice "mix" of covers and had a fair number hosting both species.

One such cover was Last Chance, which earned its name at the end of a cold November day. We had moved a good number of grouse in various bushes and by late afternoon Len had four while I had three, plus several woodcock. On our way home I asked if he knew of one more spot we might try. He thought for a few moments and said "There's a cover a few miles down the road but it's our last chance."

The sun was casting long shadows when we entered the covert and nothing moved until we came to an overgrown field of hawthorn bushes. Barney went on point at the edge of a particularly large clump and, as Len moved in one side, the grouse roared out the other, and was promptly dumped. This filled Len's quota. We went on further and Barney again stiffened near some haws. This time I moved forward alone and was presented with an easy straight-away. It was now getting chilly and, as dusk was approaching, we reluctantly headed back to the car. We had covered most of the distance when Barney made game off to our left and eventually went rigid. Knowing this would be my final opportunity, I was tense as I neared the twin haw bushes. To my dismay, the grouse made his getaway exactly in line with the bushes and blocked my vision. Dashing between the prickly trees I caught a glimpse of his departing stern and just managed to tumble him with my second barrel.

Ever since that day the cover has been known as Last Chance.

Thinking of Last Chance reminds me of another incident concerning woodcock. Len and I had a standing arrangement to hunt every Sunday, which we augmented with weekday outings whenever we could get away. One particular Sunday I awoke to a howling gale and shortly after got a call from Len saying it would be useless to hunt. As this was in the middle of the woodcock flight and I didn't want to lose a precious day, I begged and cajoled him into giving it a try.

Our first stop was Last Chance. As we walked into the cover, branches crashed from the trees and we had to tug our hats over our ears to keep from losing them. It was a dreadful day for upland gunning. However, we moved woodcock, lots of them. Curiously, the birds were either "speed merchants" whipped away by the wind, or, if they chose to buck the tempest, easy "floaters."

Grouse are hard to come by on a windy day and this was no exception. The only one we saw was flushed by the report of Len's 20-gauge when he smacked a woodcock. The grouse broke 30 feet ahead and climbed straight away. More by good luck than good management, my load of 9's caught up with it nearly 40 yards out and killed it instantly.

Last Chance is a large cover and it took us three hours to work it, but by the time we left Len had his limit of woodcock and I was short one 'doodle but had a grouse. That day taught us wind was not necessarily a deterrent to good woodcock shooting.

Another time, we entered a cover at the corner of two dirt roads and bumped a grouse. We barely had time to load our guns when the bird zoomed past Len and headed straight for me like a No. 8 skeet target. Without thinking, I flung a shot at it in self-defense, but missed as my glasses clouded. Pivoting, I peered through the murky lenses and caught the grouse with my second barrel as it crossed the road.

My lenses clouded because the bird had excreted as it passed over and I caught the full load on the bridge of my nose and my glasses. A Scottish friend told me that if a bonnie grouse treats you in this manner it's good luck. I hope so!

Grouse seen prior to flight have always caused me grief. It is especially difficult when they launch themselves from a tree. A few years ago, while hunting woodcock, Shane treed three grouse in a stand of poplars. The sun backlit the yellow leaves and the grouse were illuminated against a golden background. At the scene, I realized I would have to move if I was to have half a chance on the flush. The inevitable happened and they rocketed out while I was en route.

When an unseen grouse swoops out of an evergreen, over my head, it is a great challenge and if I connect it is noted carefully in the Log.

One of the great lifesavers of woodcock is the alder limb. Countless times my swing has been aborted, and I have been left muttering oaths as the 'cock twittered away. When shooting in sumac bushes your gun can brush most branches aside, as they are very limber. So the next time you flush a bird in the sumacs, continue your swing and the branch *may* yield!

Woodcock get me in some of the damndest predicaments. Last fall, Shane put one up that I couldn't shoot at, but fortunately it landed nearby. Hurrying to the spot through the brambles I stumbled into a hole. As I started to fall forward, the woodcock jumped. On the way down I managed to mount my gun and get a shot off before measuring my length in the briars. The result was quite a few scratches, but I bagged the timberdoodle.

A slow shot, I need every advantage to get "on" the

bird. The solution to the problem is gun mounting. There is only one correct position when a flush is anticipated: the gun should be pointing *forward* with the muzzles at head height and the butt against your midsection. If you go in at the popular "port-arms" position you needlessly handicap yourself. I know I'm not good enough to do that.

Some days your partner will get all the shooting. On other days the reverse will be true. My partner and I have always tried to share the shooting equally. It helps to know that a grouse is more likely to flush to cover, while a woodcock is inclined to head for the open. This guideline has helped us to predict who is most likely to get the shot and let us change positions.

When Len moved away I not only lost a hunting partner but also the services of his good dog, Barney. As a result, I didn't visit the coverts as frequently, but still made sporadic sorties with my Labrador. Hunting with a flushing dog is a different proposition than shooting over one of the pointing breeds; yet Shane and I have always managed to find birds. Over the years we have had a lot of fun together.

Shane was introduced to grouse at the floatplane base near Mattagami, on our way to James Bay. The owner of the little air service had a camp on the lake about 200 yards from the main dock. While we waited for the weather to clear Shane wandered off towards the camp. Shortly after I heard several shots from a .22 but thought nothing of it. A few minutes later there was a commotion down the shore and, looking in that direction, I saw a strange procession. Shane was in the lead, carrying something in his mouth, and running behind him were four youngsters and Mr. Pronovost, all yelling excitedly.

Shane reached me a few moments later and proudly

delivered a fine fat grouse to my hand. The rest of the entourage panted up and, as soon as Mr. Pronovost got his breath, I learned the story. Apparently he had been shooting "perdrix" from his front porch and one had been lost. The sound of the shots attracted the dog who, unbidden, quickly found the bird. Mr. Pronovost was so impressed he offered to buy Shane on the spot!

Shane is deadly on woodcock — his nose is excellent, and he obviously likes their scent. In the uplands, timberdoodles are his specialty; he usually puts them up within gunshot and *never* loses one.

He has also been responsible for good grouse days, although he will bump birds. When partridge are skittish, he has a knack of flushing them towards me. That may be luck, but nevertheless it happens with some consistency. I remember a wily old cock bird that lived in the most frightful blackthorn and cedar morass. I was on one side of a wall of cedars when Shane flushed it on the other side. The bird hurtled in front of me and, alerted by the noise, I was able to center him just as he darted through a gap in the cedars. Had I been alone it is unlikely the bird would have moved, and if it had, it would have been out of sight on the other side of the evergreens.

Woodcock covers disappear for a variety of reasons, but the overwhelming cause is urbanization. Most followers of the longbill experience anxiety each fall when they revisit favorite haunts, lest they find a house or trailer has pre-empted the ground.

This became an acute problem after Len's departure, and I was faced with the task of finding new covers. The first year of prospecting made me painfully aware that I didn't know as much about the timberdoodle's environment as I had previously thought. Clearly, I needed a crash course on woodcock habitat, so I turned to my old friend Ray de Ruette.

Ray is a tall, spare Belgian who came to Canada at the end of World War II. His knowledge of game is incredible and he is an excellent teacher. Ray loves grouse, but his favorite bird is the woodcock. Both of us feel that once the ground has frozen and the woodcock have departed, something special is missing from the upland scene.

Ray is a man of strong convictions. One of them is the firm belief that a dog is not necessary when hunting timberdoodles. He backs up this statement by *regularly* filling his eight bird limit without canine assistance.

Ray and I hunted together all one fall, and by the time the "freeze-up" came I could instinctively recognize woodcock cover. It is one thing to send your dog with a wave of your hand to investigate a likely stand, but quite another to walk the ground yourself. When two men are hunting longbills without a dog, thoroughness is the key, and each prospective bush is appraised with the calculating eye of a Dutch diamond cutter regarding a difficult stone. A basic point that Ray drummed into me was to hunt the edges. This proved itself time and again and applies to most, if not all, upland work. I walked countless miles, but I learned. Surprisingly, the Log indicates I shot nearly as many birds as when out with a pointing dog, but the effort was much greater. One of the main drawbacks of hunting woodcock this way is the number of birds you flush but cannot reflush, despite your knowledge of the approximate area where they landed. Downed birds are another problem and although we lost very few, some took considerable time to find.

The exercise was worthwhile from an educational point of view and has helped me ever since. It also confirmed, beyond question, that woodcock shooting is much more enjoyable (and productive) with a dog.

Game farms serve several useful purposes. They provide an environment for dog work, an opportunity for the experienced shooter to sharpen his eye on feathered game, and a place for the novice to shoot his first birds under controlled conditions. The mainstay of a typical shooting preserve is the ringnecked pheasant. Some also have quail, duck and chukar partridge.

The first time that John and I visited a game farm was about 15 years ago. Len Baillie was one of the proprietors, and looked after us with his German Shorthair, Duke. On that occasion, Len compared our performance to two kids let loose in a candy shop. Having only shot wild game, we were amazed at how easy the lumbering pheasants were to knock down. Before the afternoon was finished, we had accounted for 19 birds with an expenditure of exactly 25 shells.

Subsequent hunts at three well-run game farms in Upper New York, and a like number in Canada, tended to confirm my initial impression: pheasants, shot over a point, on a game farm, require little skill other than the ability to hold your fire so that they will be edible when struck.

Another method of shooting pheasants is the tower shot. Birds are released from a tower surrounded by gunners, with the object of simulating "driven" pheasants. If the tower is sufficiently high, and there is a good wind, mature birds can provide relatively sporty shooting. I have participated in a number of tower shoots at which we normally released 100 pheasants for eight guns. To permit the ringnecks to reach maximum speed, we stand at least 100 yards back from the tower. As pheasants prefer to fly with the wind, they invariably favor a certain section of the circle. To allow for this we move clockwise one "position" every fourth bird. On an average day, 12 to 15 birds might successfully run the gauntlet. At the end of the shoot we flushed the missed pheasants with our retrievers — the phase I found most sporting.

Quail on preserves, like pheasant, should not be compared with their counterparts in the wild. However, I have had challenging quail shooting on captive birds in Southern Ontario near Peterborough. These bobwhites were raised in giant pens and were released in late summer. My visits were usually in November, and by that time, the birds were well acclimatised, relatively wild, and very strong flyers.

The first time I spotted a covey on the ground, I thought the dog was pointing a cowpad, until the brown mass disintegrated like a land mine, and a dozen quail scattered!

My favorite bird on the preserve circuit is the chukar partridge. I like his dash and élan. When he lifts off, it is at full speed, and a fast swing is required to catch him. When hunting him I always use my Labrador rather than a pointer to guarantee spontaneity.

I remember one particular incident from some years ago. Shane struck scent in a patch of millet. By his action it was obvious he was on to a bird. Moments later the chukar erupted and was dropped. Shane obediently raced to the fall, picked up the bird and started back. On his way he made a sudden detour and veered towards the millet again. Another chukar sprang into the air and met the same fate as the first. Shane then proceeded to the second bird and, dropping his initial charge, picked up the latter one. Realizing something was wrong, he reversed the procedure, but each switch left one bird on the ground. Finally, with great care, he managed to get them both in his mouth and proudly returned to me.

Turning back to wild game; for a number of years we

had outstanding Hungarian partridge shooting within 30 miles of Ottawa, near Winchester.

I was fortunate to be invited shooting a number of times by men who had excellent, wide-ranging dogs. The "Hun" is a fine gamebird, but the method of hunting him left something to be desired.

The coveys were dispersed over a large area of cropped fields and corn stubble. Each day we walked endless miles without a break, unless the dog, who was usually at least one field away, went on point. When this happened we would race to the scene. Inevitably, we were in poor condition to shoot, and missed more than we should.

Sadly, the Hungarian partridge population has suffered a severe decline. Two hard winters in a row and over-shooting have been the cause. The area attained such fame that hunters with caravans of dogs came from all parts of the continent. These "experts" were mainly responsible for the excessive gunning pressure, as they went through the fields like vacuum cleaners.

Ptarmigan are very sporty birds. Their flight style resembles their cousin the ruffed grouse, and like him they are superb eating.

My first "formal" ptarmigan hunt took place with Jimmy Williams at Winisk, on Hudson Bay. We hunted over a stretch of muskeg near the airport. Muskeg is a mossy type of bog peculiar to the Far North, whose yielding surface makes walking exhausting. There were lots of birds in the relatively small area, but the nature of the terrain made every step an effort.

During the afternoon we staggered through the muskeg under the direction of Philip, our Cree guide, while Shane bounded ahead, flushing cackling ptarmigan to right and left. I would be less than truthful if I said we shot well; nevertheless, by 4 P.M. both of us had our quota of five birds. It was strenuous but exciting, and I remember it fondly.

Sharptail grouse are normally found around Winisk in the fall, but that year the migration was late and we didn't see any birds. I have however, literally "dropped in" on a bunch of sharptails. The incident occurred at Camp Shilo in Manitoba. I landed in the middle of a covey at the end of a parachute descent; I'm not sure who was the more surprised.

Reviewing my days in the uplands, a number of home truths come to mind, although some took a long time to learn.

A basic factor which can influence your ability to get on target is the way you hold your gun. Proper gun mounting is half the solution to hitting a fast disappearing bird. Hold the gun pointing forward, with the muzzles at eye level and the butt near your belt. A short lifting movement puts the butt into your shoulder, with the result that you are looking down the barrels at the mark. This "carry" is worth adopting whenever you are in "birdy" terrain, and especially valuable when approaching a point.

Silence is the golden rule in the uplands. Observe it from the moment you arrive at a cover. Even shut the car doors quietly, as both grouse and woodcock favor the edges, and many are found close to the road. Once in the bush, communication can be maintained by a simple two-note whistle.

We have found it most effective for two men to work parallel. A fluorescent hat is a great help in locating your partner. A fluorescent hat *and* fluorescent vest are even better. Brushy fencelines, clumps of berry bushes and blowdowns should be inspected with one gun on each side. This way, one or the other is usually assured of a shot, regardless of the direction the bird chooses to exit. If you are both on the same side, invariably the quarry will flush on the other. The only exception would be a particularly dense stand of alders or similar foliage. In this case, take turns going into the morass as a "beater," knowing that the only person to get a shot will be the man standing in the open. Frequently the bird flies deeper into the cover, but it works often enough to make the gamble worthwhile.

Some people like to smash through the brush, while others move slowly and quietly. I favor a slow basic pace, with stops at clearings and fencelines. However, when confronted with dense vegetation I try to speed through it, resuming a sedate pace when the trees thin sufficiently to swing the gun. Pausing at fences, and stamping your feet *before* crossing the obstacle will sometimes flush a bird. A good number roared to freedom at the creak of the wire before I learned to observe this precaution.

Grouse are notorious "runners" and ill-considered noise will often precipitate them into a footrace — with you as the loser. Woodcock have a reputation for sitting tight, but they too will run. Most hunters have experienced a succession of non-productive points which eventually culminated in a woodcock being flown. Frequently, the dog was pointing the same bird, but it kept on moving. A few seasons ago I was surprised to see a timberdoodle scampering over some bare ground — I hurried after him, but the little rascal made good his escape.

Woodcock habitat is usually low ground, typically alder bottoms. However, if we don't find them in the alders we change our tactics and work the hillsides, particularly stands of birch and poplar. Often we locate them on the *high* ground. Grouse like the sun after a cold night and will usually be found at the edge of clearings taking a sun bath. Over the years, I have come to realize that a light rain or drizzle doesn't deter the prospects for grouse hunting. However, a heavy downpour will drive them into the sheltering evergreens. Another negative condition is a high wind—the birds seem to be unstrung by the rattling leaves and clicking branches, with the result that they flush out of range.

If you raise one grouse, it pays to be on the alert for another one to jump. I try to refrain from shooting at distant birds, as too often I have wasted both barrels, and then had a bird rise within good range. This is particularly common in the early season, before the coveys have dispersed, but also occurs later in the year. When you shoot at a partridge it is prudent to reload *immediately*. Last November my brother John and a friend moved a grouse from under a berry-laden clump of hawthorn bushes, which they shot. Within the next 30 seconds *four* more came out singly, and all but one fell to their guns. Had they not been alert to the possibility of a multiple flush, they might only have bagged the first "pat."

Grouse shooters are divided as to whether you need a dog or not. The argument seems to revolve around the number of birds you will put up with each method. Setting that question aside, I must observe that, as a retriever, no man can match a dog. Only last year I was out with Ray de Ruette, who is the best "non-dog" hunter I know, when he knocked a grouse down in heavy bush. Both of us went to the fall, which revealed numerous feathers leading to a slash-covered ravine. We didn't get the grouse, but I am *certain* most dogs would have. Cripples can often be detected by the way the birds fall. If the bird folds its wings and drops like a stone, count on a dead grouse. A ragged tumble from the sky usually indicates a broken wing, and you should get to the scene as quickly as possible.

Both grouse and woodcock require a fast swing. In many instances, you have no time to take a "line," but must snap or throw the shot. This technique calls for a light, well-balanced gun with short barrels. Double guns are the logical choice. Over-and-unders are fine, but I prefer side-by-sides, as their broad twin tubes help to align the mark. While speed is essential, *haste* is to be avoided. In my case, it has saved the life of many a game bird. One considered shot is more effective than two hasty ones; most birds will give you sufficient time for one good shot.

The majority of grouse and woodcock are dropped within 75 feet of the gun. For woodcock, 50 feet would be more accurate. For this reason, I like an upland gun — bored cylinder and improved cylinder, or skeet and skeet. A light, open choked gun, throwing a dense pattern of small shot, is a deadly combination. For woodcock, the standard No. 9 skeet load is perfect, while 7½ trap is excellent for grouse. Early in the season, when you are likely to encounter both birds, skeet loads will suffice, but No. 8 trap loads are a better compromise.

Once the bird is in hand, there is the problem of preserving it for the table. Woodcock keep quite well, but grouse spoil quickly (particularly if they are heavily shot, or feeding on skunk cabbage). The best solution is to draw them in the field. Some people use a piece of coat hanger with a U-bend as an instrument to remove the entrails. By accident, I discovered that a stainless steel tablespoon works even better, and a *teaspoon* is perfect for woodcock.

You don't need a heavy game bag to be happy in the uplands.

chapter 7

Crows

The crow is a challenging adversary who will test both your wits and your markmanship. His habits have earned him the reputation of being an avian gangster.

Rather than launch into a tirade against crows, I will simply mention that they are the enemy of all songbirds. A 1946 survey by Ducks Unlimited found them responsible for the demise of 30 million ducks. Lest you worry that the balance of nature may be upset by shooting them, the crow population has increased over the last 30 years, while the reverse is true for most of their feathered brethren, especially game birds. Winter comes early in my part of the country, and crows provide the only opportunity to use a shotgun during the long hiatus between seasons.

Crows return to our area at the beginning of March, a time when the fields are blanketed with snow. They tend to concentrate in garbage dumps. We knew this, and being familiar with the drawing power of a stuffed owl, thought the combination of an owl and a dump would be surefire. Accordingly, we obtained from Hector Bedard a mounted great horned owl and fastened it to a sectional 12-foot steel pole.

Our first outing was at South Hull on March 19, 1961. We built a small blind in a wood on the fringe of the dump and, at precisely 8:30, erected our owl. The morning was not a success. We hailed every bird we saw during the next three hours, but our calls were ignored. The five crows we did shoot were ones that took us by surprise.

Realizing that something was wrong with our technique, we paid a visit to Hector Bedard a few days later. Hector advised us to get some crow decoys and to set up at dawn. In addition, we were cautioned to use our calls sparingly.

After numerous inquiries, we finally located a retired woodcarver who agreed to make a dozen oversize crow decoys and promised delivery the following week.

At dawn on March 25, we returned to the South Hull dump. By 10 A.M. we had shot 11 crows, and it was obvious that Hector's advice had contributed to our success. In particular, we noticed that the crows would approach the owl with confidence if we remained quiet, and from that day on we left our calls at home.

The following Saturday we built a blind of stumps at the base of a tree on Oscar Durocher's farm, near Thurso. When we returned the next morning we were laden like pack mules. John carried the owl, our guns, and the indispensable haversacks, while I staggered under the weight of our new wooden crow decoys. Upon reaching the site we were faced with the task of hanging the decoys in our tree. This we accomplished by throwing weighted lines over the limbs, which permitted us to hoist them into place. The exercise had its moments of frustration, but once they were all up the effect was impressive.

Our blind was located on the lip of a ravine, surrounded by acres of flat pasture. Because of this position, we had a panoramic view of the countryside which allowed us to spot approaching crows from any direction.

The only drawback was the wind, which made our decoys bump against each other with a clicking sound like giant castanets. This caused us little concern until one of them came crashing down and destroyed part of the blind, which gave us quite a turn, as each decoy weighed five pounds! Realizing that we could be the next target, we realigned two that were suspended directly above us.

Notwithstanding the decoy hazard, we had a nice morning, and it was particularly exciting to have the crows spot our rig from a distance, and then make a beeline for the owl. By the end of the day we had accounted for 17 of the black rascals.

That spring we had one more shoot on Monsieur Girouard's farm. Our blind was located at the corner of a field bordered by tall conifers. We chose this site because there was a large heap of manure that had, as its centerpiece, a dead shoat perched like the cherry on an ice cream sundae. The crows evidently regarded the ill-fated pig as the pièce de résistance. For this hunt we set our decoys on the ground and, at John's insistence, placed several near the hindquarters of the shoat.

To be in position by sunup, we rose at 3:30, but it was worth it. The early breakfast crowd arrived at 4:45 and we were there to greet them. The flight continued intermittently, and by 12 noon we had downed 21 of the ebony marauders.

That summer I was introduced to another type of crow shooting known as "stop and call." Practiced for years throughout the continent, it requires no equipment other than camouflage clothing and a call. In this method, you drive the back roads until you see a likely looking bush. Having concealed the car, you hide yourself and call the birds to your position.

In mid-June I was invited by two friends to do a circuit for crows on the Quebec side of the Ottawa River. My host had a piece of equipment I had never seen before— an electronic caller, consisting of a portable turntable and an amplifying horn.

Knowing that crows prefer to approach against the wind, the amplifier was pointed downwind, while the guns formed a triangle with the operator at the apex. This setup was deadly. Having only shot crows on a "passive" basis, I was amazed at the way the call would infuriate them and bring them storming in at treetop level. During the day we made 17 stops and bagged 61 crows.

As soon as I returned to Ottawa I gave John a full report on the success of the electronic call, and we ordered one the following winter.

During the early months of 1962 we laid our strategy for the spring crow campaign. Our plan was to have a "string" of dumps we could hit on successive weekends during the peak period. To this end, we drove endless miles in January and February reconnoitering dumps within a 50-mile radius of Ottawa.

A military "appreciation" is the assessment of all relevant factors in a given situation, which are then correlated to form a successful battle plan. Old infantrymen, we applied the same principle to scouting the dumps. In our case, the first question to be satisfied was the number of crows using the area. To find this out it was necessary to visit the sites early in the morning, before the crows had been disturbed. If there were a good number, we would then obtain permission to shoot from the dumpkeeper and, at the same time, inquire about the dumping schedule, so that we could return on a quiet day. Once this was in order, we would spend several hours walking the ground and watching the birds. We needed to know the favored entry route, the resting area, and the principal flight lanes. The prevailing wind influenced the siting of the blind. In this connection, we preferred open patches, as crows come in at treetop level and a stand of dense growth would obscure the owl. We tried to locate the hide as far away from the refuse pile as possible for two reasons: first, human traffic, if far enough away, wouldn't interfere with the shooting; and second, the smell! Before leaving, we always took a few minutes to socialize with the dumpkeepers. To a man, they were great characters, and before long we were on a first name basis with a good number of them. In those days, a "Sunday drive" meant bundling my young daughters into the car and checking out the nearest dump.

As crows are great carrion feeders, we reasoned that if we could acquire a dead horse, and place it in a good spot, we would have the makings of a "bonanza" shoot. Accordingly, we passed the word to a number of our farmer friends to keep us in mind if one became available. On February 17, Oscar Durocher phoned John to say that one of his mares had succumbed to old age and we could have her carcass. A few weeks later we drove up to Oscar's and, after a conversation with Monsieur Girouard, it was arranged that "Old Bess" would be placed in the field with the manure pile, in the position formerly occupied by the shoat.

To say that we were optimistic would be an understatement; we considered Old Bess our key to a 100-bird shoot.

During that winter our equipment was augmented and refined. The heavy wooden decoys were replaced by 12 plastic ones which were not only a joy to carry, but much easier to loft. They could be thrown directly into a tree while attached to a spool of kite string. For shooting in the snow, we acquired army surplus white smocks and trousers as well as white winter boots known as muk-luks. Because most of our shooting was done from the kneeling position, we bought pads of Styrofoam. These proved a boon on many a cold morning.

Our first shoot was on March 18, at the Masson dump. As there was virtually no cover we dug a shallow pit in the snow and, dressed completely in white, including face masks, were invisible to the crows.

The face masks remind me of an incident that occurred the previous afternoon. I had just returned home from buying several yards of white tulle and, anxious to check whether I could see through the gauzy fabric, draped it over my head. At that moment my daughter Julia, who was then about three, came into the living room and found me staring out the window under the veil of tulle. Her brown eyes widened at the apparition, and fleeing to her mother, she asked "Is Daddy going to be a bride?"

To return to the Masson dump. From the outset, we enjoyed a steady trickle of birds and, confident the shoot-ing would continue, decided to experiment with our setup.

During the morning we split our decoys into two groups and quickly noticed that the way they were sited had a marked effect on the crows' approach to the owl. We had read about "hangers," a pair of dead crows joined at their necks by a two-foot cord, and tried them for the first time. We hurled two pairs of "hangers" into a tree on our left flank and were impressed at how lifelike they appeared when buffeted by the wind. The crows were impressed too, as several decoyed to the flapping cadavers rather than to the owl. We also learned that a downed crow, in the open, can upstage your owl. We discovered this when we heard a bunch of crows making a commotion behind us and, thinking they were mobbing an owl or a fox, I went back to investigate. I found a dead crow spreadeagled on the snow.

We subsequently learned that on any big shoot a number of apparently unharmed birds will drop a long distance from the blind and, if it's open country, they must be retrieved or the shooting will suffer.

By noon we had 36, and as the flight had pretty well stopped, we decided to pick up. In crow shooting the "pick-up" is literal, in that you should not only remove the "hangers" but also retrieve all the fallen and bury them. This serves a twofold purpose: first, it removes any reminder for the crows; second, it leaves no trace for humans—the way you might pick up your spent shells in a favorite woodcock cover. Dumps will usually only stand one big shoot, and if the area is bothered frequently, no one gets any sport.

On our way home from Masson we made a long detour to check on the status of "Old Bess."

Unfortunately, Bess was frozen solid and there wasn't a crow within a mile. Close inspection revealed that she had not been touched by a single ebony beak, but this was not surprising as even a woodpecker would have had trouble getting a snack.

Drastic action was obviously needed if we were to save the day. Our bedside consultation ended with the decision to return the following Wednesday, with our axes, to perform cosmetic surgery.

Our next shoot was at the Aylmer dump, which occupied 30 acres on the north edge of town. The day

before, we made a careful reconnaisance and decided to
locate our blind in the northeast corner. This was a good
choice, as it was on the incoming flight line, and yet far
enough away from the refuse pile. However, it lacked
cover. Except for a few haw bushes, there was nothing.
Nevertheless, we dug a shallow kidney-shaped pit in the
snow, 30 yards from the fence which marked the eastern
boundary. On the other side of the fence, open fields
stretched away to the horizon. As the prevailing wind
was from the west, we sited our pit facing east, and
centered it between two small trees growing in the fenceline. These trees were particularly important, as they
allowed us to flank the owl with decoys, once it was
lashed to a fencepost.

The next morning was a crisp 25°, the sky was clear,
and a northwest wind stirred as we crunched over the
snow to our blind. It was already pink in the east and,
realizing we were late, we hurried to hang the decoys. By
the time the last one was in place, a number of dark
shapes had circled our position, and raucous calls could
be heard from several quarters.

Within minutes, the first crow came in low, directly to
our front, and as he neared the owl he emitted a gutteral
"CAAAA!" Two seconds later he was dead. From then
on we had fast shooting. Most would approach from the
open fields and pass between the decoy trees, presenting
a classic head-on shot. Others floated in on stiff wings,
without a sound, less than 20 feet above the snow. It
was easy shooting, as our white outfits made us invisible,
and the first bird was usually folded before he realized
anything was amiss. We mounted our guns with stealth
to avoid flaring the birds; a mandatory technique if you
shoot without cover.

It was a thoroughly enjoyable morning and we encoun-
tered only one problem—the rising sun. As we faced due

east, by 7 A.M. we were looking straight into a fiery ball, whose brilliance saved the life of a number of black bandits. However, we got our share, and were delighted with our bag of 65 when we picked up at 11 A.M.

On April Fools' Day we hit the Templeton dump. The terrain presented a challenge in the construction of a blind as it was flat and sandy, due to the removal of topsoil. However, a few dead trees were still standing, and we built a sparse blind in the exposed roots of one. As the previous week had been unseasonably mild, most of the snow had disappeared, which prompted us to switch to regular camouflage clothing, including net face masks.

The morning was overcast, with light snow blown on a northwest wind. In the early hours the flight was steady, but by 8 A.M. our shooting tapered off. We noticed that birds which we missed, or which flared out of range, made their exit in the same direction each time, and this gave us an idea. Our plan was to split up, with one staying in the blind, while the other stationed himself on the "escape route;" this way we could catch them both coming and going.

To test our theory, John went 100 yards downwind and crouched by an undercut bank while I remained in the blind. A few minutes later a pair decoyed to the owl. I shot one, while John picked off the survivor as he winged down the "escape route."

When a pair of crows decoys, they usually employ a technique that wartime fighter pilots used. The lead bird comes in low, while his partner follows behind at a higher altitude. This presents a problem in making doubles, as the "tail end Charlie" is usually out of range when the first bird is dumped. The "escape route" ploy solves this problem.

Crows flare violently at the report of a gun and keep

up their aerial acrobatics for 30 or 40 yards before resuming level flight. Therefore, a gun on the escape route can expect fast flying, but relatively straight targets. That morning, John made a number of doubles on overhead "screamers" that were a joy to watch.

By splitting up, we were able to shoot as many birds *after* 8 A.M. as in the early hours, despite the reduced air traffic. We remember the Templeton dump as the birthplace of a new technique that was to help us immensely in the future. When we picked up at 11 A.M. we had 64 birds.

Because there were still a lot of crows working the Aylmer dump we decided to try it again at the end of the season. We returned on April 15 and, as the snow had gone, located our blind 150 yards west of the fence. Most of the crows had forgotten our previous visit, and decoyed beautifully. The heavy wind made shooting quite tricky, but by 8 A.M. we had downed 27 birds. I mention the bag by 8 A.M. because we found, over the years, that we could estimate the total for the day by doubling that figure.

From 8 A.M. on we split up and, utilizing the escape route technique, made the most of a dwindling flight. When we left at 10:30 we were happy to have shot 54, because it is very unusual to get two good shoots from a dump in the same year.

We saved "Old Bess" for the last shoot of the year, as we wanted to finish on a triumphant note. With high hopes and a half case of 7½ trap, we returned to M. Girouard's field on April 21. To make sure we wouldn't miss any, we arrived in the pitch dark and were completely set up before first light. The morning was perfect, with a good west wind, and we were certain of success.

By 8 A.M. we had shot all comers, and out total bag

was two birds. Bitterly disappointed, we packed up and decided to try some of the nearby bushes with our electronic caller.

The first prospect was an isolated bush, flanked by fields and backed by a dense stand of timber, one-quarter mile in from the road. Somewhat depressed by the failure of "Old Bess" to produce, John opted to take movies rather than to shoot.

When we reached the spot we found we were on a little knoll ringed with evergreens. While I knelt at the edge, John pointed the amplifier downwind, toward the forest, and started the "riot" call.

Within three minutes we had our first visitor, whose demise was faithfully recorded on film. Before he had hit the ground, a pair appeared over the treetops, and one tumbled in a puff of black feathers. The action continued fast and furious with birds screaming in from all directions. Fortunately, I was shooting well, as John had turned into a tyrant behind the camera lens and was barking orders as to precisely where he wanted the birds shot. If one approached from the side I would immediately hear something like "Let him cross the opening and shoot him on the way out!" or "Shoot him now, he's backlit!" Used to receiving instructions from my older brother, I did my best to comply.

Eventually, the crows had enough, and when a complete playing of the "riot" call failed to attract a single bird we turned the machine off. John and I then gathered the fallen for burial and were surprised when we counted 24; I was even more surprised to see I had only fired 31 shells.

From the end of April to mid-June we stopped crow shooting because the birds were nesting. One shouldn't do "stop and call" before the young can fly, as there is a good chance both parents will be shot. When the young are in the nest, adults respond with abandon to any call, and while the crow is a gangster, I don't want to appeal to his parental instincts, nor do I want the young to starve.

In our area, the young are on the wing by June 10. To be on the safe side, our first venture that year was on June 20, which yielded 70 crows. Two weeks later we got 63. We didn't go out during the rest of July or August, as it was too hot, but made a "circuit" on Labor Day, which produced one interesting incident.

Near the hamlet of Ladysmith, we spotted a good bunch of crows feeding in a grain field. As this was open country we had to drive a considerable distance before we located cover — a dried out pond, surrounded by 30-foot poplars. We left the car 100 yards up the road and, returning to the swale, hid ourselves before turning on the call. The crows took some time to reach us, but finally appeared over the trees. As usual, we let them come in until they were at point blank range and hammered the first few right above our heads. Then, spontaneously, we started to take them over the poplars, roughly 30 yards away. Finally, we were dropping them as soon as they came into view. The result was three clearly defined rows of dead crows; the first at our feet, the next in the poplars and the last on the far side of the trees in the field. We shot 14 at that stop, and bagged a total of 60 for the day.

The electronic caller had a short-term attraction for us, and we dispensed with it the following year. We didn't like the artificiality of using a record player nor the constant racket, which prevents one from savoring the day.

During the winter we tried for one goal — the elusive 100-bird shoot. We not only checked out the dumps of the previous year, and tried to assess when each would be "ripe," but also prospected for fresh locations. Three new dumps were added to our "string"—Thurso, Buckingham, and Ste. Rose. The first two were promising, the last one a question mark.

The season got underway slowly, as the crows seemed to dawdle on their northern migration. Our first shoot was on St. Patrick's Day, at Buckingham, and we got 35. The next weekend, we shot Masson and picked up 20, while the following Sunday we shot 16 at Aylmer. This disastrous start suggested the next shoot would produce eight to ten. But it didn't.

The Ste. Rose dump was next on our agenda. This dump was difficult to find because it was hidden in a valley, and its unmarked entrance was through the dumpkeeper's yard. The valley ran east and west, with an average width of 100 yards. One end of the ravine was blocked by dense conifers, while the other led through a woodcock bush to a broad open valley. We located two small blinds which faced north, but backed onto the scrub-covered south slope.

We were set up in Ste. Rose by 5:15 Sunday morning, April 7. The temperature was 30° and the day promised to be clear, with a northwest wind.

Initially, it looked as though we were in for a poor shoot as there was no "dawn patrol." However, the crows began to trickle in steadily in ones and twos, and by 8 A.M. we had 51.

For the rest of the morning we split up and used all our resources and cunning to outsmart the crows. Twice during the forenoon the wind shifted, and so did the "escape route." By 12:05 P.M. we had 99 and were down to our last shell. By this time the flight had stopped and the warmth of the sun, combined with our early start, made us groggy with fatigue.

Finally, after one hour, we sighted a single crow flying

in to the dump from the north. The bird spotted our owl and, lowering slightly, headed right in "on the beam." This was a classic overhead opportunity which we had made many times earlier in the day, but under the present circumstances, it presented a formidable challenge.

I held my breath as John mounted his Webley, and started tracking the crow. It was a "pressure" situation. At the last moment, the gun roared, and the crow collapsed; we had done it!

Successful crow shooting calls for a degree of care and preparation similar to that required when hunting Canada geese.

As with Canadas, you must first locate your quarry, which in the case of crows means a thorough check of dumps, rural abattoirs, and grain fields. In addition, it pays to keep a continual watch for a crow flyway. When you spot one, trace the route back to its source. Here a word of caution is in order: most flyways terminate in a roost, but the roost should *never* be shot. If you shoot in a crow roost you may effectively ruin your hunting for the future. This is tantamount to strip mining the Mother Lode. Instead, place your blind some distance from the rookery.

Regardless of where the birds are located, the site of your blind should be chosen with great care. First consider the flight line which the crows use to enter the area. Once this has been established, assess the prevailing wind, which should be at your back. Third, note the height of the surrounding foliage, as crows come in at treetop level. A good decoy rig can lure the birds within gunshot. We have found an owl and 12 crow decoys to be the best combination. Use a mounted great horned owl, or try to procure as lifelike a replica as possible. The quality standard for crow decoys is not as critical as for the owl, and the full-bodied plastic models are excellent If you have to touch up the finish on your decoys, remember to use *flat* paint (this applies to any type of decoy).

The owl should be sited prominently, within good range of your blind. A telescopic pole for the owl can be very useful. Crow decoys show to their best advantage when lofted high in nearby trees; however, if the terrain is treeless they can be placed on the ground to good effect. For decoy shooting, a call is *not* necessary.

Whether you shoot from a blind, or engage in "stop and call," camouflage clothing, including a face mask, is *essential*. Initially, you may consider the face mask a nuisance, but it will neither impair your vision nor your gunpointing.

Typical shots you are likely to encounter will be low incomers, high crossers, and wildly flaring birds. Incomers are easy—just blot them out, keep swinging, and pull the trigger. Crossers and high overhead shots should be executed with a free swing and treated like passing ducks. At the sound of your gun, a crow can describe some incredible gyrations in the air, which transforms each one into a challenge. I use an abbreviated swing or "snap" them—and sometimes it works. Perhaps the best advice is not to hesitate, but to fire as soon as you are "on" the bird.

Any gun that fits you will do for crows, providing it's not too cumbersome, or tightly choked. We prefer our short-barreled, open-bored upland guns. The crow is surprisingly frail and can't carry "lead," so the standard 7½ trap load is ideal, and ensures clean kills. The mild recoil will not punish you if your gun is not properly mounted—which happens frequently during a banner shoot.

While some may scoff, the crow is a great gamebird, and there is much to be said for a good spring dump shoot.

Tom Hennessey

chapter 8

The Shitepoke Duck Club

The outstanding appeal of the Shitepoke Club lies not only in the fine shooting, but in the relaxed camaraderie. Our namesake is the Shitepoke or great blue heron, a majestic hallmark of many good duck marshes.

The Shitepoke Club was formed in 1967, upon the acquisition of a 280-acre marsh from Quebec Hyrdo. Our constitution reads:

> "The purpose of the club shall be to provide a natural habitat to encourage the population of wildfowl, and to provide a camp and buildings where members may enjoy the pleasures of hunting. To this end, the members shall assist and cooperate with the game wardens, and other proper officers of the Province of Quebec, within the boundaries of the property of the club."

The founders were John, Roger Rowley and myself. John and I had known Roger since childhood, but had seen him infrequently due to the demands of his military career. He had been our guest at Stuart Molson's and we had recognized in him, a "kindred soul." When Roger retired in 1967 he had no established shooting ties, and it was natural that he should join us in a gunning partnership.

Our new lease from Quebec Hydro was located on the western boundary of the Black Bay Duck Club. It resembled a shallow lake, with a deep border of reeds. To the north, the ground sloped sharply to the highway and, to the south, a narrow spit of land separated the marsh from the Ottawa River.

During that summer we had a prefab erected on the south shore in the center of our property. The camp had a narrow porch, four tiny bedrooms and a large main room, with picture windows facing the marsh. Our stove, fridge, and lights were operated by propane gas, while heat was provided by a Franklin stove. As there was no running water, we brought five gallon jugs each weekend, and used an outhouse discreetly located some distance from the camp.

To watch over the property, and assist us with the chores, we engaged Gerard Legault. Gerard was one of Joe's sons, and owned a farm which overlooked our marsh. As some of his cattle grazed on our land, he visited the camp every day, an arrangement that worked to our mutual benefit.

At the end of July, Gerard reported that trouble was brewing with our old friend M. Labonte. This was the same Labonte with whom we had clashed many years before on Presqu'ile. Apparently, Labonte had leased a section of our north shore from one of the farmers and planned to shoot in our marsh.

We tried to reason with Labonte, but were ignored until we sent him a lawyer's letter. This produced a threat from him to "spite bait" our property. Spite baiting is a nasty trick involving the dumping of grain in a marsh, followed by an anonymous "tip" to the authorities. According to law, the officers have no choice but to close the marsh.

In desperation, we called the R.C.M.P. to explain our problem and received a courteous hearing but little comfort.

Finally, to resolve the matter, we submitted to a form of blackmail and "bought" M. Labonte's lease.

Prior to the Opening, we purchased two 12-foot Vercheres boats and had "push in" cedar blinds built to accommodate them. In addition, our old box blind was refurbished and staked in position.

Our first Opening was a great success. Roger occupied the box blind off the island known as Point, John was in the open water at Channel and I was near the north shore at Corner. We had our limits and were back in camp by 8 A.M.

This was just as well, because we had a steady procession of visitors throughout the day. I should explain that in French Canada, the Opening of the duck season is regarded by many as the equivalent of Christmas, New Year's or St. Patrick's Day, possibly all three. The guest book was signed by a total of 12 visitors (including the game warden) and most signatures still defy recognition.

A few days later John and I went to James Bay and Roger had Barbara, his wife, down to the camp for the weekend.

Saturday morning they crossed the marsh to Corner blind, which was located near the north shore. Shortly after sunup, two cars stopped on the highway and *seven* poachers descended the hill and fanned out along the edge of the marsh. These people were recent immigrants and when Roger yelled at them he was greeted by a salvo of gunfire. Enraged, Roger pushed the boat out of the blind and poled furiously towards them, pausing only long enough to load and fire. Barbara in the meantime, was lying in the bottom of the craft. Initially, the poachers fired back, but as the boat drew closer their ranks broke, and they fled up the hill to their cars.

Roger treated the whole affair rather lightly, but Barbara's day was ruined. However, when John, our president, learned of the incident he immediately awarded Roger the Order of the Golden Shitepoke (2nd class) with "V" for Valor.

Poachers notwithstanding, we had very good shooting, and during the weeks that followed the marsh gradually revealed its character. Point blind was best at the beginning of the season or when there was a strong west wind. Corner was productive until the freeze-up, and attracted blacks and mallards. Channel was also a consistent producer, and the first choice for ringbills. The only drawback to the marsh was the early freeze due to the shallow water. By November 1, we were through. That first season we shot 13 different species of ducks, including a pair of canvasback.

Early in 1968 we entered into prolonged negotiations with the Quebec Hydro, to acquire a block of their surplus land upriver from our lease. In April of 1969 we purchased a 300-acre tract three miles east of Masson. This was a superb location, only 17 miles from Ottawa.

The property encompassed a section of Lochaber Bay, which was an inlet running parallel to the Ottawa River, consisting of flooded benchland. The dominant feature was the bay, which appeared as a channel running from east to west with a deep border of weeds on both shores. From the air, our tract was shaped like a parallelogram, with a tag extending north from the river to Highway 8.

Because of the extent of our new holding, and the substantial capital outlay, we decided to invite one more person to join us.

David Wright was our first choice, as he was a long-time friend and ardent gunner. In addition to being a fine companion, he had a variety of skills and a special feel for the outdoors. He also possessed a great sense of humor and delighted in teasing with a straight face. On all counts, he was a most welcome addition to the club roster, which was amended to read:

> John R. Woods—President
> Major General Roger Rowley—Vice President
> Shirley E. Woods—Honorary Secretary-Treasurer
> David F. Wright—Member

By the spring of 1969 we had two duck marshes. The one we had leased was fully operational, while the new one was a vast stretch of promising but undeveloped real estate. Naturally, our decision was to give up the leased property and concentrate on our new holding. It was impossible to move our old camp, so we arranged to sell it. We included our boats and blinds as well as the basic furnishings, which meant that we had to start from scratch in setting up our new camp.

We were very lucky to have the Bouwman brothers as neighbors. These men, who had come from Holland after the war, turned out to be towers of strength—each was over six feet tall and all muscle. John, the elder, had been a master carpenter before he turned to farming, and his young brother Theo had also been in the construction industry. Together, they built us a first-rate camp modeled after our original prefab but larger. Instead of four small bedrooms we had two large double rooms. When the camp was complete, Theo agreed to be our guardian, and has been an invaluable help ever since.

Our building was sited on the extreme eastern boundary in a grove of tall pines overlooking the marsh, with the Ottawa River in the distance. To reach the spot it was necessary to bulldoze a road for half a mile through the bush from the highway. The route was laid in a twisting course, to take advantage of the contours. The result was a delight to the eye and the surface remained passable in any weather, due to a series of strategically placed culverts.

Working feverishly, by August we had the road into the camp. The building was nearly finished but not furnished, our new blinds were under construction, and all our problems were solved except for how we were going to get our new 14-foot boats from the camp through the 200-yard belt of weeds to the open water.

The answer was a channel. However, our first attempt to dig one with a backhoe failed in the swampy terrain. We turned the problem over in our minds and decided the only solution was to dynamite a canal. Accordingly, we contracted for a licensed explosives expert to come down and do the job. The individual in question had little stomach for the task, and once on the ground, announced that he would need more men. Roger and David conferred briefly, and while the expert loafed in the shade they set to work.

They bored holes in the muck with a broomhandle, and then inserted 60 or 70 sticks of dynamite in a row. The last stick was then detonated with a plunger and the whole line ignited in sympathetic reaction. The project took over 1200 sticks, and there were some glorious explosions. By the end of the day, a boat could run from the camp to the open water with reasonable ease. A few hours work by the backhoe put the finishing touches on the harbor.

That first season we staked our box blind within 50 yards of the mouth of the canal and named it Home, while the two "push in" blinds were located on the opposite shore of the bay. One "push in" was anchored near an old stump and was named Nituk's Stump and the other was placed at the southwestern corner of the property.

I missed the first Opening because I was at Winisk, goose hunting, but the Log records it was a dandy, and everyone had their limit by 9 A.M. The following Saturday, October 4, I went with Shane to Home blind for the evening shoot. Traditionally, the weekend after the Opening is slow and this one was no exception. By late afternoon I had only managed to scratch down a ringbill and a black duck.

Just after Shane retrieved the black, my eye was caught by movement down the marsh and, looking to the east, I saw seven geese heading my way. A few seconds' study confirmed that if they maintained course, they would pass right over the blind. Crouching low, I rummaged for some goose loads, but the best I could come up with were high brass 6's. A glance through the cedars revealed the Canadas were drifting off to my left. Realizing it was now or never, I stood up and, with a generous lead, pulled on the nearest bird. The goose folded, quite dead, so I swung on to another, which subsequently cartwheeled into a tall stand of weeds behind me. Roger was across the bay in Nituk's Stump and sent a loud halloo of congratulations across the water.

Shane picked up the first Canada quite easily, but spent a considerable time in the dense jungle of bullrushes before he emerged with the second one. Waiting on the outside, my anxiety mounted as the minutes ticked by and I was thrilled when he finally appeared with the goose.

The evening finished on a high note when I dropped a

pair of bluewings with one shot, just before sunset. As a result of my good luck that day, the blind was renamed Coltrin's Corner (after my street).

The first season was a success in many ways. Our marsh disclosed its secrets as the weeks went by. We spent a considerable amount of time exploring the ridge and experimenting with various blind locations.

The ridge, a low spine of land, rose from the marsh on our south shore and ran parallel with the main channel. On the north side, facing our camp, was a 100-yard belt of weeds which grew in knee-deep water. On the south side, which faced the Ottawa River, the water was deeper and the vegetation more extensive. We referred to the south side as the Rice Paddies and soon learned it was a great holding area for ducks. At the eastern end of the ridge was a flooded section of dead trees which we called the Pinoaks. The Pinoaks reminded us of pictures we had seen of duck shooting in the lowlands of Illinois and Arkansas.

That year we had limit shoots from both sides of the bay with Coltrin's Corner and Nituk's Stump the most consistent producers. In addition, we found there was excellent jump shooting on the north side of the ridge, as well as pass shooting on it when the conditions were right. Most encouraging, our marsh didn't freeze until late November, and this not only extended our season but gave us a crack at the northern redlegs.

That winter we purchased a 30-acre block which adjoined our eastern boundary. This was vital for protection as our camp was within 100 feet of the line. In addition, it was primarily bush, with terrain that lent itself to the construction of a pond. A deep fold acted as a collecting basin for water draining in from a wide area. Because it was boggy, there were no trees, and we knew that a dragline could strip the overburden with no difficulty.

During the previous fall we had noticed, as the season progressed, that a great many ducks sought refuge from the wind by settling in the long grass which bordered the bay. With this in mind, we also made plans to build a pond in the swamp pasture on our shore, roughly one-quarter mile west of the camp.

On June 17, we supervised while M. Boucher and his dragline dug out a pond on our new property. This required a delicate touch on M. Boucher's part, as he had to go deep enough to remove all the topsoil, but not deep enough to penetrate the underlayer of clay necessary to retain the water. The resulting slough had a little island at one end and was roughly 250 x 100 feet. The pond was christened Rogie's in honor of our vice-president.

The next day, M. Boucher made a similar pond for us in the open marsh, which we named Willow, in recognition of the surrounding scrub.

On June 21, Roger and I went down to the camp and lovingly hand-seeded the raw edges of both ponds with red clover and alfalfa. The clover sprouted within a week.

The Opening was very brief for me that year as I had to be in Montreal for a wedding that afternoon. Fortunately, I was able to be there for our traditional dinner the night before, and enjoyed a nice shoot the next morning in Coltrin's Corner.

Shane and I arrived at the blind at 7 A.M., full daylight, as I like to watch the flight of ducks on the Opening as much as I like to shoot them. To permit my dog to see the birds and mark the falls, I propped the door open in the cedar blind; this didn't scare the ducks and even the wary blacks maintained their course. I shot mostly ringbills that morning as the "big ducks," early in the season, have a lot of pinfeathers. I did have one black, a high bird that I couldn't resist trying.

The new ponds produced very nicely and, during the weeks that followed, each of us got a limit from both

Rogie's and Willow. My first shoot in Rogie's was with a good friend, Don Sperling, who comes up for a hunt each fall from New York. We went into the pond at 7 A.M. and, shooting without a blind, had our quota within an hour. Included in the bag were several wood-ducks which Don and I, as fly tiers, regarded as special trophies.

Willow Pond was baptized by John and me on October 31. It was a typical overcast late fall day with an east wind. At the outset, we noticed a difference in the way the birds reacted to the open pond, as compared to Rogie's, which was surrounded by trees. Despite the fact that we remained motionless, ducks were reluctant to decoy and we soon found that the best policy was to take them on their first pass. We had a steady flight, all blacks and mallards, with the exception of our first visitor, a green-winged teal, and picked up our decoys at 9:30.

At one point in the morning, a heavily-hit black scaled down 200 yards away and landed in some heavy thorn bushes near our camp. Shane lit out after the bird and, upon reaching the area, started working a patch which we were quite certain was at least 30 yards from the fall. Just as I was about to leave the blind and direct him, he picked up the dead duck. This was one of many in-stances where my dog knew better than I, and it pointed out once again the wisdom of letting the retriever use his own judgment.

In the intervening years, our initial impressions of the ponds have been confirmed. Rogie's comes "on stream" early in the season and the birds tend to decoy, while Willow is best late in the fall, and unless there is a spanking west wind, provides mainly pass shooting. The ponds have another special appeal for me—they offer a decent environment for the dog to work. Out in the bay, ducks (including blacks and mallards) will often dive or swim away with just their bill above water, thus eliminating any scent. When shooting in the ponds I never worry about losing a cripple, but in the bay it is an entirely different matter.

Understandably, we are interested in our property, and each year try to do something to improve the habitat for ducks. The next spring we planted 20 ten-foot poplars and a pair of weeping willows around the pond in the marsh to provide a windbreak. This project took a lot of heavy labor. Even our president joined us in the task of digging holes in the hard clay. Unfortunately, only ten survived, including the two weeping willows, and even these have not grown as quickly as they should.

Because the camp was located at the eastern edge of our holdings, we tended to concentrate our hunting in that area, but realized we were neglecting the western section. In addition, our channel required constant maintenance and was often the cause of sheared pins. After two years, it was obvious we should relocate the camp. The logical site was Oak Point, a spit of land crowned with lovely old oaks which bisected the north shore of our property. As Oak Point extended to the water's edge, it gave us direct access to the main channel, and was equidistant from our east and west boundaries. Unfortunately, at the time we didn't own Oak Point, but this problem was overcome when our good neighbor M. Larose agreed, after some persuasion, to sell us the land.

At the beginning of August the camp was dragged on skids by M. Laniel's bulldozer to the new location. Once it was in place, and set on concrete blocks, we examined the interior and were delighted to see it had survived the journey without a crack; mute testimony to the Bouwmans' workmanship and Laniel's skill.

At the same time the building was moved, we had our

road extended for half a mile along our northern boundary to the new location. The construction of a sturdy dock directly in front of the house completed the transfer.

Standing on the porch we have a panoramic view of the marsh and the channel. Despite our proximity to Ottawa, there is scant trace of civilization, and the loudest noise to be heard is the cry of a gull or the distant quacking of ducks in the reeds.

The interior is partitioned into one long multi-purpose room with picture windows, which occupies the front of the structure. Two double bedrooms take up the rear. Entering, the cooking and dining area is to the left, and the living room is to the right. On the wall, near the door, is a fine gunrack made by David, which holds the double guns favored by the members. Old "family" rugs cover the linoleum floor and hunting prints hang on the walls. The bedrooms are sparsely furnished, but functional, and include a stand for a candle over each bed.

As with our original prefab, the lights, stove and fridge are fueled by propane, and we have neither running water nor a telephone. The Franklin stove throws a lot of heat, and while the bedrooms remain rather chilly, we can raise the temperature in the main room from below freezing to 55° to 60° within an hour. Our privy is located in a grove of trees and permits a view of the morning flight through the open door. The squirrels like our privy too, and insist on shredding the toilet paper to make nests; in self-defense we keep the roll in an old cookie tin.

We have been very happy on Oak Point. The Log reflects our good fortune:

10 Oct. Tues. 39°
R.R. & S.E.W. drove down to John Bouwman's at

7:15 P.M. armed with shovels; thence to his back cornfield where we worked diligently in the frosty blackness, digging two pits. Arrived back at the camp at 9:30, interior temp 42°, and gas had run out. After considerable work, particularly with the fridge, all systems go, fire crackling in the hearth, and hopes high for the morrow! Our plan is to shoot geese in the A.M. and try Rogie's Pond in the P.M.— as Willow is reserved for DFW and JRW this weekend. The pits will be known henceforth as Les Oies and may be *rented* by John or David for a nominal fee of $5, per pit, per diem.

11 Oct. Wed. 38°
Cloudy, NE wind. Set up in Bouwman's at 6:45— first birds appeared at 7 A.M. Four flocks inspected our rig (which should be larger) but we fired on only two occasions. S.E.W. doubled on Canadas and we picked up at 10 A.M. with three geese. On the way in to camp we flushed at least 200 blacks and mallards out of Willow. In addition to the puddleducks, there are a tremendous number of ringbill in the bay. We agreed to try Rogie's for two hours, from 11–1 P.M. and then return to Bouwman's field for the evening flight. Rogie's had at least 100 birds (mostly large ducks). We waited for the blacks and mallards to return, which they did in a steady procession, about one hour later. We had our limit at 12:45—three blacks and nine mallards, and the birds were still pouring in! There is no doubt the cold snap of 7–8 Oct. has blown a tremendous number of birds down — those in Rogie's were definitely "northerns."

I write this on the side steps of the porch and Roger insists I watch at least 50 birds circling, in groups, to come into Willow — it looks like O'Hare field! A fine day—the camp is a paradise with both the ponds and the marsh loaded, plus the geese.

The foregoing lacks modesty and would not qualify for a Pulitzer Prize, but indicates the type of sport we sometimes have.

That season was very good, as was the succeeding one; both were relatively uneventful except for little things such as the loss of a cedar blind in the spring breakup, or the discovery of bear droppings around Rogie's pond. But our idyllic existence was nearly interrupted by tragedy a few years ago, one late October day.

Roger and I had Don Sperling and Jimmy Williams as guests while John and David were goose hunting in James Bay. On Saturday afternoon, Roger took Don to Coltrin's Corner, and I set off with Jimmy, half an hour later, for Nituk's Stump.

As there was a raw wind and the temperature was 40°, both of us wore plenty of heavy clothing under our chest waders and parkas. The boat we used was a light metal, square-ended "john boat," 12 feet long, partially decked-in with a platform covering the bow.

As usual, Shane perched on the platform while I ran the motor, and Jimmy, knees to his chin, squashed himself in the space between us. Because of the cramped quarters, Jimmy cradled his brand new Browning O/U and my new Churchill in his lap. As there was a slight chop, I proceeded down the bay with caution.

Suddenly, Shane shifted his weight, the bow caught a wave, and the boat slewed under. Realizing we were going to swamp, I bellowed "Help!" and turned for shore, but it was too late. We sank like a stone, but within moments the boat popped to the surface, upside down. Jimmy also went under, but he too reappeared, and greeted me with the words "My gun's lost but I've still got yours." As we were in 20 feet of icy water, my gun seemed an academic consideration.

Initially, we had six inches of freeboard to hold onto, but lost most of it when Shane tried to climb atop the overturned boat. The next time he tried to climb the hull I gave him a whack with the oar. He could swim, but for us it was life or death. By this time Roger and Don were trying to start the boat, but the motor wouldn't catch. Our predicament was serious — we had no buoyancy, due to the heavy clothing, shells, and chest waders, and we were just able to keep our faces above water by holding the few inches of freeboard remaining at one end with our fingertips.

Eventually, Roger and Don reached us, but they had to row and it seemed to take an age. Roger later said that he could see us going down, and had visions of telling our wives. When he did reach us, we were waxy-faced and blue-lipped — the water was only a few degrees above freezing. Because Roger's boat was already overloaded, we were towed to shore, and it was a long cold slog back to camp.

In the Log I noted that I had committed three gross errors of water safety. The boat was not only unseaworthy, it was also overloaded; we had worn chest waders *under* parkas with shells in them; and we didn't even have a life preserver *between* us, let alone one for each person. Since then I have taken considerably more care on the water.

A few weeks later John and I had another boating experience, which though not potentially fatal, could have resulted in considerable discomfort.

Again, it was a Saturday afternoon and we were alone at the camp. A gale was blowing from the west and, as we wanted to shoot the far side of the bay, we gassed up our old fiberglass trimaran "whaler." The result was a stable, mobile blind. With the 3 horsepower motor on the stern we made slow but steady progress across the channel to the opposite reed bed.

When we picked up our decoys at the end of the afternoon, we found that the motor wouldn't start. An attempt to row back to camp against the wind broke an oar, and this mishap caused us to lose control of the craft. With only one oar, the heavy wind caught us and we were pushed down the marsh in the gathering darkness at an impressive speed until we bumped into the Pinoaks.

Our only hope at that stage was to try to attract the attention of someone at the Lovell's duck camp, half a mile to the east. We fired the international distress signal (three evenly-spaced shots) but got no reaction. Eventually, we gave up, and resigned ourselves to a night in the Pinoaks — an unpleasant prospect, as the mercury was falling but the wind was getting stronger.

Just before dark, Phil Lovell, who had been in a blind on the opposite shore, spotted us on his way home and, turning his big boat, crashed through the whitecaps to our position. We were awfully glad to see him. It would have been a long cold night.

These incidents are fairly typical of boating mishaps associated with wildfowling. Duck hunters, as a group, are exposed to all the normal water hazards *plus* seasonal high winds and low temperatures. My own mistakes have taught me some valuable lessons.

Probably the most important thing I have learned is to respect cold water. Approach any given boating situation cautiously. Faced with the option of a short rough route, or a long safe course to my destination, I choose the latter every time.

All boats should have reserve gear aboard; this can range from a spare paddle in a duck skiff to an extra 10 horsepower motor in a big launch. Flashlights, tools and spare parts all come under this heading.

Cushion-type life preservers should be checked frequently, as they can become waterlogged and permanently compressed. When this happens, they should be re-placed, as they lose buoyancy. Provide at *least* one life preserver for each occupant. Today, there is a wide variety of personal life vests, flotation jackets and buoyant hunting coats on the market. The one you choose should be tested under controlled conditions be-fore the season opens. If you decide on a CO_2 inflatable model, remember to allow sufficient room for it to *expand* when activated — it is best to wear this type *over* your outer clothing.

Several outdoor writers have stated in print that chest waders permit one to swim quite easily. I disagree. In fact, my "test" convinced me that chest waders are a tremendous liability and *extremely* dangerous.

Hip boots are not as great a hazard, but it is prudent, when boating in deep water, to unstrap them and roll them down below your knees. This will allow you to kick them off at a moment's notice.

One final observation; the "buddy system" has long been recognized in water safety, and hunting with a companion is not only more enjoyable, it may save your life.

Each of us has a mental picture of ideal duck shooting conditions. With John and me, it is when the marsh is stark, and snow is in the air. That year we closed the season on just such a day.

The temperature was 28° when we broke the ice in Rogie's Pond and set out six feather decoys. Our sur-roundings were beautiful — six inches of fresh snow and the strengthening sun gave the area a pristine brilliance.

However, it was a full hour before we had our first visitors, a flock of 25 blacks and mallards. These birds circled three times and then descended into the decoys en masse. As we don't shoot at flocks, there was nothing we could do but stay hidden, and flush them out by clapping our hands. This happened with two more large bunches and finally, we decided to shoot at the next flock.

The ensuing two hours produced not only classic shooting but some truly impressive sights of blacks and mallards as they entered the "snow bowl."

It was a glorious finish to the year, and I had one of the pictures I took that day of Shane retrieving a drake mallard made into a Christmas card.

In a real sense we feel our marsh entails responsibility and consider it a trust for the future. The annual Wildlife Service band has confirmed that the improved property supports more ducks now than when we purchased it. We have not acted purely from unselfishness, however. The truth is we enjoy the challenge immensely and wrangle each winter as to whose pet project will be implemented. For example, while we shoot woodduck infrequently, we have noticed a decline in their numbers recently. As a result, two years ago we imposed a ban on the species, and plan to build nesting boxes to help bring them back.

My favorite time at the camp is Friday night, particularly the moment when I blow out the candle by my bed. Once the candle is out, I see the flicker of the firelight on the living room wall and, before I am lulled to sleep by the sighing wind in the eaves, I give Shane a final push to assert my territorial rights.

The cares of the week are forgotten and my thoughts are of the morrow.

chapter 9

Guns, Clothing and Equipment

Guns, clothing, and equipment are topics sure to provoke controversy at any gathering of gunners. In this chapter I express opinions that I have arrived at from personal experience. It is *not* my intention that you regard the following as a definitive treatise. Rather, I ask that you consider it as one man's views which may be of interest.

At the outset I would like to stress that inexpensive, plain guns *kill* every bit as well as highly engraved custom models. Further, I am certain it is academic to the bird, when it is struck by a load of chilled shot, whether the charge was fired from an English Purdey sidelock or an Iver Johnson single-shot. The end result is the same. If you shoot *well* with a mass-produced gun, and *enjoy* using it, there is no need to fret about upgrading your weapon. Both my father and Jack Heney used Winchester Model 12 Trap guns, bored full choke, for everything from geese to woodcock, over a period of 40 years. They could easily have acquired more prestigious weapons but, as they shot brilliantly with their long-barreled pumps, they saw no reason to change.

Experience leads me to believe that the most reliable and best balanced shotgun is the double-barreled side-by-side—it has been tested and perfected over two centuries. The side-by-side is closely followed by the over-and-under; but the O/U is a heavier weapon, and lacks the racy, classic lines of the side-by-side. Both are excellent for all species of game, but especially valuable in the uplands, due to their balance and pointability.

Automatics or autoloading shotguns contain a mechanism which ejects the spent shell, thrusts a fresh cartridge into the chamber, and cocks the action. These functions absorb a substantial amount of recoil, so that a light "kick" is felt when the gun is fired. Mild recoil is a great virtue of the autoloaders, and has made them a favorite of the skeet shooting fraternity. While countless game birds are shot each fall by automatics, this type of gun would not be my choice. Compared to doubles and pump guns, they are cumbersome and heavy, and some are prone to malfunction.

The pump is a good compromise between the automatic and the double-barreled gun. It has the firepower of an automatic and *some* of the balance and reliability associated with the double. In my estimation, the Winchester Model 12 stands head and shoulders above all others in this class.

Regardless of the gun, I recommend a well padded "sheath" type case with an exterior covering of *porous* fabric (canvas) and a full-length zipper. This type can be opened and completely dried after a wet day, while those with a waterproof outer shell tend to retain moisture. Any weapon stored in a damp case will suffer serious damage.

I was brought up in the belief that the only "man's" gun was a 12-gauge, with 30-inch barrels, bored full choke. Indeed, when I was 15, I used the first money I ever earned to buy a Winchester pump, Model 12, which conformed to these specifications.

However, when I was 17, Dad gave me a Browning Superposed with 28-inch barrels, bored full and improved modified. It replaced the pump gun, and became my most cherished possession. Although it weighed over eight pounds, I shot all the species of game mentioned in this book with it and put literally thousands of rounds through it. For some time it has been retired, but I take it out occasionally, when faced with the prospect of long-range shooting.

Over the years I tried a representative variety of guns, but none really appealed to me as I had become a staunch double-barrel man in general, and an over-and-under fancier in particular. In the early 1960's, I bought two more Browning Superposed guns, one a 12, the other a 20; both were the Lightning model, and both were bored improved cylinder and modified. In time, the lightweight, open-bored 12 became my standard gun for waterfowl, while the 20 was used for crows, snipe, and upland game.

In Spring, 1970, I made arrangements through Abercrombie & Fitch to receive coaching from Rex Gage, senior instructor of Holland & Holland, the famous British firm of gunmakers. I hoped that he would identify and correct some of the faults in my shooting style that had accumulated over the seasons. Rex was a superb teacher, and the half day I spent with him taught me a great deal. In this connection, I should mention that a lesson from a British shooting coach is an opportunity one should not pass up. One of the key things I learned was the importance of proper gun mounting; a factor we are inclined to treat rather casually on this continent.

Most of the 250 rounds I fired were from his double-barreled, side-by-side "try gun." This weapon, by its very nature, lacked balance and looked like a plumber's nightmare, but once it was adjusted to fit, I broke claybirds with it consistently. For the first time, I realized the pleasure of a "straight hand" grip and the ease of sighting along twin tubes. When the tutorial ended, I had in my pocket two pieces of paper; one contained updated measurements for the stocks of my over-and-unders, and the other was a set of specifications for a new double-barreled side-by-side.

The seed was planted, and it was only a question of time (and money) before it would germinate and send me to London in quest of a British side-by-side.

A few years ago I had a financial windfall which precipitated a trip to England. At the time, my wife was led to believe that the jaunt was nothing more than a spur-of-the-moment holiday, but expressed some curiosity as to my choice of London in midwinter, rather than the Caribbean. The answer was, of course, that I wanted to buy a gun. Before leaving Canada I wrote to eight of the best-known gunmakers to advise them of my interest and pending visit.

We arrived in London on a Saturday and the following Monday I made a circuit of all the firms. The first seven were most courteous, but the story was the same; they had no second-hand side-by-sides with 2¾-inch chambers. They would build one, if I cared to wait from two to seven years! My last stop was Messrs. Churchill, Atkin, Grant & Lang on Bury Street.

Once again, my inquiry drew a negative response but, as I turned to leave, the managing director indicated he might have "something." This "something" turned out to be a "best" sidelock, with a single trigger, which had been started the year before. The gun was far from complete, but had the basic components; a rough block of walnut inletted to the action which was, in turn, fitted to the "white" barrels. Because the man who had ordered it had died, the gun was for sale and could be finished for delivery in less than one year. As it had a single trigger it was exactly what I wanted and, although the price was staggering, I bought it, sight unseen.

The next stop was the West London Shooting Grounds, where I spent an intense morning being fitted under the watchful eye of David Rose. It was my aim to have a gun that I could use for everything, which meant relatively short barrels; in this respect I was lucky to have chosen a Churchill. As some readers may know, the late Robert Churchill was the originator of the 25-inch barrel gun, for which he designed a special high tapered rib which produced the illusion of a longer sighting plane. I knew the short-barreled gun would be ideal for the upland shooting, but was not sure I could use it on high birds requiring a sustained lead. This question could only be resolved by shooting clays from the high tower with two "try guns;" one with 27-inch barrels, and the other with 25-inch tubes and a Churchill rib.

After the initial fitting which was done by shooting at whitewashed steel plates, we repaired to the high tower. The West London Shooting Grounds have a number of towers from which clays are thrown to represent various species of driven game. The platform on the highest was 120 feet above ground (equivalent in height to a ten-story building) and we stood back from it roughly 100 yards. It was quite a test. The birds were thrown by a high-speed trap and first appeared as a tiny speck until they flashed overhead looking about the size of a dime. Under the guidance of my instructor, I broke an acceptable number with the short-barreled gun, and he assured me that 25-inch barrels would be a sound choice.

The next day I returned to Churchill's and spent several hours going over minutiae connected with the "bespoken" or custom element of my gun. To illustrate the thoroughness of a good gunmaker, I will mention that we spent at least ten minutes discussing the size of my hand as it related to the circumference of the grip and the space required from comb to tang. The only deviation from classic British specifications was a slim semibeavertail fore-end and an unobtrusive butt pad. The barrels were to be bored to print improved-cylinder and quarter-choke patterns with standard American 7½ trap loads.

In August of that year I took delivery of my Churchill XXV, serial number 8705, and was delighted with the finished product. As I had hoped, the result was an all-round gun, and since then I have proved it on a wide variety of game. Its lightness, balance and "pointability" make it a treat to handle, while the engraving and workmanship are a joy to the eye.

The gun was expensive, but I received, as the English say, "Value for Money," and it is a purchase I have never regretted.

Over a 25-year period, I have swung from long-barreled, heavily choked guns to light, short-barreled, open-bored weapons.

There is a simple logic behind this change. I have found that the latter not only puts more game in the bag, but is much more pleasant to handle. At the same time, I have come to realize that pattern is more important than penetration and as a result, favor standard loads of relatively small shot. I should add that I won't knowingly shoot at a bird more than 40 yards away, as I hate to cripple them. If you *measure* 40 yards, you will find it is not a restrictive distance.

For the record, the following are my favorite loads. The sole criterion for their choice is the efficiency with which they kill:

SPECIES	SIZE OF SHOT	LOAD
Geese	2	1¼ oz.
Puddle ducks	6	1⅛ oz. 1¼ oz.
Diving ducks	6	1¼ oz.
Grouse, chukar, huns & ptarmigan	7½	1⅛ oz. Trap
Pheasant	7½	1⅛ oz. Trap
Crows	7½	1⅛ oz. Trap
Woodcock, snipe,	9	1⅛ oz. Skeet

Speaking in general terms, I think that on this continent we are inclined to use too much gun, too much choke, and too much shot.

Turning to equipment, I would like to discuss outdoor apparel. My family have been manufacturers in this field since the turn of the century. Therefore, I can speak with some knowledge.

As a general rule, when dressing for the outdoors, try to wear lightweight garments, with as little bulk as possible. The reasons for this are obvious; heavy clothing will sap your energy and impair your swing, while bulk will ruin gun fit.

Starting at the ground, let us first consider footwear. I prefer leather boots with non-slip soles for cruising the bush. The sole of the boot is the key to remaining upright while negotiating uneven terrain, and the best I have found are the deep-cleated variety. Despite numerous attempts to waterproof my boots, no preparation has sealed out moisture for the whole day. However, wet feet are a small price to pay for the comfort and support that leather provides. During the season I rotate two pairs and *always* keep shoetrees in them.

Picking burrs and seeds from my socks used to be a tedious ritual after a day in the coverts. Now I wear nylon gaiters which were originally designed for hikers and cross country skiers. Not only are they comfortable, but they really work!

For wildfowling, I usually wear hip boots, and find the fabric-topped ones superior. They are light, supple, and do not bind your legs when sitting for an extended period. Dampness inside waders and hip boots is an ongoing problem. The answer, I have found, is to wear removable felt insoles, and use electric boot dryers at night. Boot dryers are inexpensive and do an excellent job. Having tried and discarded a number of insulated boots, I finally settled on the felt-lined type favored by snow-mobilers. For sedentary hunting, such as later-afternoon duck shooting, they are perfect.

I wear heavyweight wool socks both shooting and fishing, and find their bulk provides a cushion as well as insulation. In upland boots, I wear dress stockings under a pair of 3½-pound wool socks. Because the leather leaches, I never wear white wool as it will inevitably stain.

Knit cuffs on hunting trousers are a great boon if you spend a lot of time in hip boots or chest waders, as I do. Tapered "stag" pants with a zipper serve the same purpose. All my lined trousers are cut this way, which is neat and prevents the material from "creeping" inside your boot.

For upland shooting I wear pants with a cotton or

nylon duck facing — both will turn aside briars and thorns. The cotton duck is cool, but sops up water; the nylon is light and nonabsorbent, but very noisy. Take your choice. Often, I compromise by wearing cotton duck pants with chaps. My chaps are made of nylon with a neoprene lining, and can be rolled up to practically nothing. I keep a pair in the game pocket of my vest all season, and they weigh no more than a woodcock. These are particularly useful on misty mornings when there is a heavy dew; once the sun dries the bush they go back in my game pocket. The game pocket also contains a pair of surgical forceps in case a dog should tangle with a porcupine. When removing quills, grasp the spine firmly and pull along the line of entry; if you try and "tweak" them out, they are likely to break and the buried stub will cause infection.

I believe the most sensible outer garment for the uplands (and snipe marshes) is a game vest. This is invariably warm work, and a vest is both light and cool. I am a firm believer in "blaze orange" or one of the other *fluorescent* shades; you won't scare the birds, but you will be seen by your partner. Recently, I nearly bagged a good friend, as well as a woodcock. My friend was wearing a tan jacket and one of the currently fashionable Irish tweed hats; this combination made him invisible in the alders. Some people like wide-brimmed hats in the bush, but I prefer the "Jones" style, which I find less likely to be knocked off when going through heavy cover.

Turning to warm clothing, I wear long underwear bottoms and a silk T-shirt. The main reason for this choice is not that I am particularly effete. Rather, the silk has little bulk, yet excellent insulating qualities, and absorbs perspiration. The Orvis Company lists silk long underwear in their current catalogue.

The best insulating material for outer apparel is down,

but I wear few down garments for shooting because of their bulk. There is, however, one exception—the down vest. My father produced the first down vest in the early 1940's. The original model was designed to be worn under a battle dress jacket and was known as the "Victory Vest." Because it has little bulk, yet wonderful insulating qualities, I find the down vest *indispensable*. When hunting in very cold weather I adopt the "layer principle" and wear several light wool sweaters with the down vest under a windproof outer shell.

John and I discovered that a pullover-type waterproof parka was ideal for wildfowling. The one we found most satisfactory has a camouflage pattern and is made by the Hodgman Company. In windy weather, a parka with a hood is the only garment which will prevent icy drafts from working their way down your neck.

As with upland hunting, I favor the "Jones" hat for duck shooting. It has a good peak, won't blow off in a wind, and fits snugly inside my parka hood.

Looking back to the uplands, I must add that I *always* wear hardened "shooting glasses" when I go in the bush. Many of my friends who don't wear them have been "twigged," and a few years ago my glasses saved me from serious injury when I was raked across the face by a thorn branch. In my opinion, anyone who hunts the woodcock covers without protective glasses is courting disaster.

On a less dramatic note, I also wear soft pigskin gloves when shooting. My business associates used to estimate, by the scars on the back of my hands, how much time I'd spent away from the office. Now they have no idea, and I don't have the discomfort of myriad scratches. Initially, I thought gloves would be a nuisance, but found after the first day that I didn't notice them.

The best bag for hunting I have ever had is a U.S. Army surplus tool carrier. This is a square-shaped haversack made of waterproof canvas. Its great advantage is the shape, which permits me to stand it upright on the floor of the boat or blind (or even the parapet of a goose pit). It has given stellar service over the years, but is finally showing signs of wear, and I wish I could find another one.

A hot cup of coffee or soup is a great restorative on a cold day. Unfortunately, the standard thermos bottle is very fragile. After breaking several dozen, I finally switched to a stainless-steel model manufactured by Stanley, and subsequently bought one made by Thermos. Both are very heavy, but virtually unbreakable, and I wouldn't be without them.

Binoculars will increase your wildfowling enjoyment immensely. Not only are they invaluable in locating and checking on downed birds, but they can enliven an otherwise dull day in the blind. I use a pair of compact Bushnell 6 x 25 binoculars. When buying binoculars, remember that it is difficult to hand-hold glasses with a magnification greater than 7X.

The mention of blinds brings up another piece of equipment which has been invaluable: a simple folding stool. A camp stool with tubular metal legs and a canvas seat has contributed to my comfort on countless decoy shoots. And the legs sink into soft ground—an advantage, as it makes the seat more stable. The stool weighs very little, and is highly portable. Another good, though not portable, seat is the metal shell box. It has an adjustable swivel seat/top which prevents muscle fatigue.

I am constantly amazed at the fearsome sheath knives some people wear when out hunting. I have been to many remote regions but have never needed to use anything other than a folding penknife. The type I like best is a Swiss model, which incorporates numerous gadgets and is made of stainless steel. A folding penknife is not as romantic (or dangerous) as a sheath knife, but, in my opinion, it is more useful, unless you plan to gut a moose, which I do not.

A question of continuing interest, particularly on distant trips, is the weather.

Some years ago I was introduced to the Pocket Forecaster. This is a celluloid dial which consists of two circular discs, roughly two inches in diameter. To obtain a forecast, one disc is set at the current barometric pressure, while the other is rotated to point in the direction of the wind. A letter of the alphabet will then appear in a small window on the face of the dial. When you look on the reverse side of the disc there is a legend beside the letter, and this gives the forecast.

My brother John, Roger Rowley, and I have used the forecaster for a number of years, in a wide variety of locations. Because of its amazing accuracy, we now refer to it as "Fearless Fosdick." To use it when traveling, I take along a pocket barometer and a compass; the whole kit can fit in the palm of my hand. The Pocket Forecaster was invented by a British infantry officer during the First World War and is *only* available from Messrs. Negretti and Zambra, New Bond Street, London. This firm handles a wide variety of scientific instruments, including pocket barometers. The Forecaster is inexpensive (less than 1£,) but a pocket barometer is quite costly.

To keep all my paraphernalia in order, I have a cubbyhole in my basement which I dignify with the name "Hunting Room." It has a metal pipe clothes rack along one wall, shelves along the other. The only furniture is a chest of drawers and a single wooden chair.

The Hunting Room permits me to keep everything in one place and, as everything is visible, the chance of forgetting an essential item is substantially reduced. The Hunting Room is "out of bounds" to everyone except my dog.

Index